Momentum Empowering Children to Read

Through Passion, Partnerships and Practice

Janine Roy

Cover photo from Shutterstock. Author photo courtesy of Teresa Y. Scribner.

Figure 4.1 is from Raschle, Nora, Réka Borbás, Carolyn King, and Nadine Gaab. 2020. Frontiers for Young Minds. "The Magical Art of Magnetic Resonance Imaging to Study the Reading Brain." https://kids.frontiersin.org/articles/10.3389/frym.2020.00072. Copyright © 2020 Raschle, Borbás, King, and Gaab. This is an open-access article distributed under the terms of the Creative Commons Attribution License (CC BY). The use, distribution or reproduction in other forums is permitted, provided the original author(s) and the copyright owner(s) are credited and that the original publication in this journal is cited, in accordance with accepted academic practice.

This book is produced in a sustainable manner.

ISBN: 978-1-915662-82-8

Table of Contents

Dedication

To my family: Robert, Matthew, Hayley, Devi, and Henry.
You are the reason for my hopefulness and urgency.

To the children, educators, and families
I have had the privilege of learning from and working with.

Introduction

*". . . (R)eading absolutely does give you a sense of yourself
in the world.
It shapes your life and opens up your life in ways nothing
else can."*

—Maya Angelou, American author, poet, and civil rights activist

Every year, I have students who I wonder and worry about. They may be shy, anxious, frustrated, challenging, or distracted. These are the kids who keep me up at night. I call these students "My Finest Teachers" because years of experience have taught me one important lesson that *they* will teach *me* the most each year. These are the students who need my enthusiasm, hard work, patience, creativity, and flexibility. But most of all, they need my love every day throughout the school year to help them start moving forward and keep moving forward in their learning. In other words, to help them have learning momentum.

Billy[1] was one of my first Finest Teachers. He was bright, inquisitive, and hyper-focused on Pokémon and

---

[1] All student names in this book are pseudonyms unless otherwise specified.

1

video games. But when it came to starting tasks he didn't want to do, like going to PE, his modus operandi was to dive under his desk, curl up in a ball, and scream continuously like a bad actor in a horror movie. His howling was loud enough to echo throughout the school. He was literally stuck under his desk, and I couldn't figure him out. In these moments, his learning momentum was stalled. And so was mine.

I tried patiently cueing upcoming transitions, setting firm boundaries, and talking with his mom—but none of these strategies worked. After repeatedly being stymied, I resorted to ineffective coaxing and eventually attempted authoritarian demands, but these were epic failures as well. His classmates were aghast at Billy's outbursts, my colleagues could hear him next door, and nothing diminished Billy's frequent explosions. I felt like a complete failure.

Finally, one day, I ignored his tirade, calmly told him I would be right back, walked the class to PE, and then returned to shrieking Billy. Knowing that the only behavior I had total control over was mine, I tried something different by quietly sitting down on the classroom floor. I discovered that my companionable silence and non-demands calmed him. Once calm, he wanted to chat. As I listened while Billy enthusiastically talked about his beloved Pokémon cards, I learned that focusing on his interests built belonging and trust with me. Then we calmly developed a plan together,

2

which taught me that he had helpful solutions if I was willing to listen, and I needed to increase my flexibility and creativity. As we chatted, I discovered that a quick connection with an adult and a quiet spot calmed him, and noisy, busy spaces like the gym were profoundly dysregulating for this anxious guy. Our solution was to schedule a daily Pokémon chat together and identify a quiet place for him to read instead of going to PE. As the explosions diminished and eventually evaporated, Billy's calmer days improved his feelings of belonging in the class, which empowered him to shift to become a friendly, Pokémon-enthusiast, hardworking classmate, and eventually a voracious Third Grade reader. While this was life-changing for Billy, this shift in my practice was transformational, as I realized that the person who had to change their behavior was me, not Billy.

Just like me, educators are the ones who need to change and do the hard work to empower Our Finest Teachers' learning momentum to help them learn to read. Our determined efforts are especially important for students furthest from educational justice. This book will lay out step-by-step systems and strategies for galvanizing students by establishing belonging, partnering with families and colleagues, and increasing student reading practice to empower Your Finest Teacher to become a voracious reader. Because literacy matters. A person's ability to read shapes

3

their survival and individuality and their future in life. Literacy affects an individual's job prospects (Poff Roman 2010), health (Somers and Mahadevan 2010), and even how well they will fare in old age (Poff Roman 2010). Being able to read thoughtfully, listen carefully, and express ideas coherently are essential twenty-first-century survival skills.

> The imperative for this book is to improve student reading through equity-driven initiatives centred on belonging, passion, partnerships, and practice.

To accomplish this monumental feat, we need heroes. While all teachers are heroes, primary teachers are superheroes. Teaching children to read requires them to simultaneously act as Sherpas (Tibetan expert mountain climbing guides), scientists, coaches, counselors, and stand-up comedians as they miraculously transform nonreaders into confident booklovers. Just as Sherpa Tenzing Norgay led Sir Edmund Hillary to traverse to the top of Mount Everest, Teacher-Mountain-Guides wisely lead young humans through the reading journey, help them navigate challenging moments, and celebrate each small step. Teacher-Scientists seek out and rely on research. Teacher-Coaches huddle up and patiently train each child to align phonics, word recognition, and comprehension. Teacher-Counselors help students manage the anxiety, frustration, and big feelings that come with a long journey. And teachers

4

are skillful stand-up comedians who come prepared every day, know their audience, and understand that timing is everything.

How primary teachers manage all these simultaneous feats with grace, determination, and a sense of humor is something that is rarely talked about. How do they transform an entire class of children, including many frustrated reluctant readers, into confident book lovers? While teachers search for professional resources on teaching reading, view educational podcasts, listen to audiobooks as they pack their lunch at night, take evening professional development courses, and scour self-help books for dealing with stress, they will find few resources that reference effective *and* efficient ready-made, research-based systems and strategies that:

- ensure every child feels belonging at school, especially those furthest from educational justice;
- foster a love of school and learning to read;
- help every child succeed in learning to read by the end of Third Grade;
- develop effective partnerships with families; and
- sustain a deep sense of accomplishment at the end of each teaching day.

This is that book.

It is essential for students to feel that they belong and are loved in their classroom and school community. They need to feel excited about what they are learning, and it is empowering for them when they see that reading practice helps them make an authentic difference in the world.

Teaching children to read requires educators to cultivate children's joy by fostering belonging, trust, and excitement. This nurtures each child's purpose and perseverance and, ultimately, their momentum to learn to read.

To do this, teachers need clear strategies to develop belonging with their students so that students feel safe enough to take risks because a child will make many mistakes before becoming a confident reader. Educators need research-based ideas for how to connect and collaborate with students and families in culturally responsive ways that address the needs of families who have been historically marginalized by school systems.

Teachers need efficient, research-based systems and strategies to help their students foster a love of school and a love of reading and build their learning momentum. At the same time, educators need to go home at the end of the day satisfied that *their* own momentum is intact but not so exhausted that they don't want to do it again tomorrow.

Being flexible and resilient is essential for making impactful pivots in life. When I've wanted something different to accelerate my professional joy or my own learning momentum, I've pivoted from changing grades to changing schools to shifting to school administration. Whenever I've been searching for something new, whether it was a new research-based strategy, a new equity-driven system, or even a new job, the person who needed to change was *me*. You, too, maybe at a pivot point in your career or your life. No matter where you are right at this moment, the key is to figure out where you want to go and how you are going to get there to initiate, accelerate, or resume your own momentum.

The 2020 global pandemic had a profound impact on every human on the planet. It caused me to make one of the biggest pivots of my professional career. In a thirty-seven-year career as a teacher, principal, and district leader in the United States and Canada, I'd worked on refining *how we teach reading* to ensure students were confident readers by the end of Third Grade. See Chapter 2 for why Third Grade is imperative. The pandemic forced educators all over the world to become instant Virtual Teacher-Mountain-Guides by leading students to shift to remote learning, traversing the challenges when students got "stuck," collaborating with fellow flummoxed teacher colleagues online, and partnering with perplexed parents to figure out how the heck we were all going to do this together. I was inspired to write this book two months after we started remote learning. Though the

7

tides of this precarious pandemic time are still ebbing and flowing, I saw clearly in those early days the *what*, and it all came down to *momentum*.

Momentum is written for educators to inspire us to do things differently! Our conversation around literacy needs to be reframed. The focus must be on working smarter, not harder. The facts around educational injustice must be faced, and we need to do something about it! Our goal is to ensure each human becomes a reader via the research-based time frame of the end of Third Grade. Because learning to read is the key to their future and ours.

Momentum is written for educators who want to work together with families to get better at what we do so we can help every child read by the end of Third Grade. This book describes *how adults can do things differently by working together to help each child learn to read*. This book removes the blame often placed on teachers, families, students, and school systems.

Momentum provides the big picture, research, and strategies for educators to build belonging, identify a learner's passions, and effectively collaborate with colleagues and families to increase reading practice so each child becomes an enthusiastic reader and a literate global citizen.

The Why, the What, and the How

Momentum provides structures, strategies, and scaffolding for creating opportunities for students to gain the momentum to learn to read. It explores the *why*, the *what*, and the *how* of building relationships, fueling motivation, and empowering learning.

This book is divided into three sections—the why, the what, and the how. Before you dive in, let me brief you on each section and its importance.

The Why

Based on the U.S. Department of Education's data, most Americans have the potential to be literate (NCES 2019a). Being literate means, they are capable of being a critical thinker and informed humans. Literacy is determined by *how adults analyze* the information, *how they think* about the information, *how they evaluate* the data, and *how they determine* a credible news source.

As one in five Americans is considered *illiterate* by the U.S. Department of Education (NCES 2019b), America has an economic, educational, and moral imperative to address illiteracy, as it has a profound impact on every human's confidence and success in life as well as a country's political climate and global economies (NCES 2019b). Literacy impacts momentum for high school graduation, postsecondary dreams, job prospects, and health outcomes.

9

While American illiteracy rates had already been an issue for decades, educational issues exploded amidst 2020's global COVID pandemic, economic crash, national, racial strife, and mental health crises. Educators, families, and policymakers were justifiably apoplectic about potential COVID-driven learning loss intensifying literacy gaps, especially for students furthest from educational justice who have been historically and systemically marginalized due to their economic background, and race, gender, and/or sexual identity.

Educational systems need equity-driven revisions, so current instructional and assessment practices require research-based overhauls. Practical strategies, tools, and guides are vital to building learning momentum to empower students, educators, and families to move forward. Chapters 1 and 2 explain the imperative of addressing illiteracy in America and the powerful pivot point of Third Grade.

The What

Momentum is the ability to start moving forward in learning and sustaining growth over time. This book shows how to nurture students' passion for reading by fostering a student's feeling of belonging and trust in their classroom, developing reading skills using research-based strategies, and partnering with families to increase reading practice at home. Combining a student's growing confidence and skills with a supportive Home–School Team builds a student's motivation, encourages their perseverance, and, as a result, strengthens their reading skills. By igniting a child's reading passions, educators build a child's learning-to-read momentum to achieve the goal of being a confident reader by the end of Third Grade.

Chapters 3 through 7 examine how to build and sustain learning momentum and explore the three key Momentum Moves.

The How

Momentum will become your practical how-to guide filled with tactics, tips, and easy takeaways to help every student learn to read.

Chapters 8 through 12 assist teachers and school leaders in strengthening perseverance through daily practice, personalized empowerment projects, and passion-centered learning to build skills and confidence.

Momentum Checklists at the end of each chapter provide takeaways on step-by-step strategies and easy-to-implement tips developed through case studies and research in the United States and Canada.

Each chapter:

- *Starts with a story!* Not only is this a culturally responsive way of learning and becoming literate but who doesn't love a story?
- *Includes research-based data* and thought-leader excerpts to empower you to know the why behind the what.
- *Culminates with case studies* that further demonstrate how the suggested techniques and practices look in the classroom.
- *Closes with Momentum Checklist:* reflections and possibilities, so you know where you are, where you are going, and how you are going to get there.

Please note:

1. *What this book is and isn't.* While this book will help you improve the reading achievement of students, it is not a tome about the art of teaching reading or a technical step-by-step how-to manual for teachers on reading instruction in the classroom. There is a multitude of brilliant research-based literacy instruction resources for teachers. See this book's 'Bibliography for How to *Actually* Teach Reading' section for recommendations.

2. *We are all in this together.* This book takes an equity-driven, inclusive, collaborative approach for teachers and

12

school leaders to improve reading. The companion guide for parents, titled *"Momentum Family Guide: Empowering Your Child's Learning While Maintaining Your Sanity and Sense of Humor* (Roy 2022)"* shares equity-centered strategies, routines and ideas with families to build each child's learning momentum. From identifying a child's superpowers and passions to helping a child self-calm, this guide helps families partner with educators to build and accelerate student momentum by increasing their reading practice at school and/or at home for a few minutes a day. These ideas are research-based and founded on 38 years of educator- and mom-wisdom, as well as field-tested and pandemic-tested by teachers, school leaders, and families. When it comes to helping each student learn to read, *Momentum Family Guide* is designed to *literally* get us all on the same page!

The Why

Each morning, I begin my workday with a quiet mantra:

Let's open their minds,
Broaden their horizons,
And teach them to read.

Chapter 1
Literacy Matters

"Literacy is a powerful liberator, leading the oppressed to self-empowerment and self-determination."

—Dr. Gholdy Muhammad, award-winning educator and author of *Cultivating Genius* (Muhammad, 2020)

Throughout this book, we will follow some of My Finest Teachers to study their learning-to-read journey.

Malik,[2] an inquisitive Kindergarten scientist, was thriving in a class by practicing reading nightly with his parents, celebrating his African American heritage at school, and proudly sharing his cultural celebrations with his classmates. His family partnered with the teacher to make sure he was reading "just right" books at home.[3] During the

---

[2] Any names used in this book are pseudonyms unless otherwise stated.

[3] "Just right books" are decodable-leveled texts at a student's independent reading level. Decodable books are "just right" when students can read 95% of the book independently. "Dessert books" are books that students are interested in and excited about, but beginning readers may find them too hard to read independently.

pandemic and once we returned to school, how could we sustain this enthusiastic reader's learning momentum?

More on "just right" books in Chapter 4.

Sophie, a highly social First Grade artist, had begun to show progress in reading thanks to her developing relationships with her teacher and peers in her new class and providing extra reading support at school and home. She enjoyed learning about a variety of cultures, as she hadn't previously explored cultures other than her own. At the start of the pandemic, she completely fell apart, engulfed by big emotions and opposing any adult support or direction. During the pandemic and once we returned to school, how could we partner with her mom to help Sophie resume and accelerate her learning momentum to continue learning to read?

Isabella, an enthusiastic Third Grade leader, was showing progress in reading prior to the pandemic due to her strong relationships with her teacher and classmates, increased reading practice, and exposure to Personalized Empowerment Projects (more in Chapter 11). She was a confident helper with younger students. She loved sharing her Hispanic heritage with her classmates. During the pandemic, she shut down due to the loss of her leadership opportunities and familiar routines. Both at home and at school, how could we get her back on track to resume and increase her learning momentum?

At the start of the 2020 Global Pandemic, along with supporting every student and family, I was especially focused on My Finest Teachers. My dedicated staff and I were hunkered down with our laptops in our homes, trying to figure out how to teach remotely when many students didn't have devices and families were facing fear, illness, and/or unemployment. Everyone was scrambling! What were we going to do? How long would this last? How would we recover educationally and economically? I felt overwhelmed and adrift. As we focused on how we could help each student in our school, I thought about the importance of every child learning to read.

The Importance of Literacy

Literacy is an essential life skill in the twenty-first century. Up front, it is important to define what "being literate" means. If literacy is defined as being able to sign one's name and complete a simple form, the United States and Canada both have inspirational 99% literacy levels. These are statistics that taxpayers can be proud of. However, looking beyond these simplistic measures of name-signing and form-completion, the Program for the International

Assessment of Adult Competencies (PIAAC), an international organization that measures global literacy skills, defines literacy as the ability to compare information, paraphrase, or make low-level inferences. PIAAC asserts that in every country, society must strive for critically thinking citizens who are able ". . . to understand, evaluate, use and engage with written texts to participate in society, to achieve one's goals, and to develop one's knowledge and potential (NCES 2019c)." PIAAC 2012 and 2014 assessments specified that 21% of American adults had low English literacy levels. The *Houston Chronicle reports that* illiteracy results in "$225 billion lost annually . . . because of unemployment, lack of workplace productivity and crime (Sessoms, n.d.)."

U.S. Department of Education research indicates that *most Americans have the potential to be literate.* They are capable of being critical thinkers and well-informed humans. It does not matter whether humans get their information via reading a book, watching a reliable newscast, or listening to a podcast or audiobook—being literate is determined by *how humans analyze* the information, *how they think* about the information, *how they evaluate* the data, and *how they determine* a credible news source. Being literate affects a human's job prospects (Poff Roman 2010), health (Somers and Mahadevan 2010), and even how long they live (Poff Roman 2010). As being able to read shapes their survival, individuality, and future in life, the ability to listen, comprehend information, consider the accuracy of the information, and express ideas are fundamental twenty-first-century survival skills.

Global pandemic or not, literacy is our top goal because *being literate impacts every human in the twenty-first century*. Literacy rates power national economies and political stability. Regardless of economic boom or bust, literacy has a profound influence on a society's endurance as it is essential for learning and thinking. Sustaining literacy determines society's capacity to survive and thrive. Equitable access to education is of paramount importance, regardless of wars, economic crises, or a global pandemic. Our schools, our country, and our global society have a moral imperative to ensure equitable access to education so the children of today will continue learning now and in the future.

Why Does Literacy Matter? Literacy impacts individuals and society in key ways.

1. *Literacy is essential for survival.* UN Secretary-General Kofi Annan said: "Literacy is a bridge from misery to hope. It is a tool for daily life in modern society. It is a bulwark against poverty, and a building block of development, an essential

complement to investments in roads, dams, clinics, and factories. Literacy is a platform for democratization and a vehicle for the promotion of cultural and national identity. Especially for girls and women, it is an agent of family health and nutrition. For everyone, everywhere, literacy is, along with education in general, a basic human right. . . . Literacy is, finally, the road to human progress and the means through which every man, woman, and child can realize his or her full potential." (United Nations 1997)

According to data cited by University of Oxford researchers Rosen and Ortiz-Ospina, if the world was 100 people, 14 of these people could not read or write. (Rosen and Ortiz-Ospina 2018). This means in 2018, 1.05 billion people were not literate—the equivalent of the combined population of North and South America not being able to read or write!" (Bridge International Academies 2019). People who cannot comprehend or compose text cannot fully participate in their communities. Being able to think critically and express ideas and perspectives on social media dominates social interactions, especially in isolated locales and global pandemics. Those who are not literate have limited life chances and lack full participation in their society and the world.

2. *Literacy shapes individuality.* What and how we think, how we perceive ourselves and others, and how we learn, grow, and change (or stagnate) are profoundly impacted by what we hear, see, read, write, talk about, and focus on throughout our lifetimes. Literacy brings joy into readers' lives along with opportunities to collaborate, think critically, and foster creativity. Being literate is a fundamental requirement for being an independent critical thinker, which is essential for our survival as educated global citizens. Literacy is an equalizing steppingstone for communities furthest from educational justice.

3. *Literacy is essential for learning.* According to the United Nations Educational, Scientific and Cultural Organization (UNESCO), literacy enables ". . . individuals to achieve their goals, to develop their knowledge and potential, and to participate fully in their community and wider society (Montoya 2018)." In her book, *Cultivating Genius,* Dr. Gholdy Muhammad writes:

21

"Literacy was the foundation of all learning. When Black people learned to read, write, and speak, they were able to accumulate knowledge in other areas and use these skills as tools to further shape, define, and navigate their lives. Literacy was not just for self-enjoyment of fulfillment, it was tied to action and efforts to shape the sociopolitical landscape of a country that was founded on oppression. . . . Literacy was connected to acts of self-empowerment, self-determination, and self-liberation." (Muhammad 2020)

If we want humans to be able to understand scientific recommendations and make informed, rational decisions when they vote, society must ensure that every person has the power to read.

4. *Literacy is essential for thinking.* During the Stone Age, survival skills ranged from hunting and gathering to running and hiding, building fires, and creating stone tools. Today, Common Core Learning Standards identify twenty-first-century survival skills ranging from comprehension to criticality and understanding other perspectives and cultures. Fundamentally, global citizens must be able to think critically to make informed decisions, which involves comparing and contrasting, synthesizing,

and evaluating both oral and written information. It is essential that all students learn to read today to sustain a productive economy and a progressive, democratic society now and in the future.

5. *Literacy impacts socio-economic status.* A person's ability to read determines their capacity to finish high school, head to college, and find a satisfying career.

   - *Finish high school.* In 2015, U.S. Census data proudly informed America that nine out of 10 adults, or 88% of the American population, had at least a high school diploma or GED (Ryan and Bauman 2016). By 2020, U.S. Census data provided more refined statistics, pulling the curtain back on the American racial disparity between white and BIPOC graduation rates that is not evident in other countries. Looking at Canada—a valid comparison to the United States of America—Statistics Canada reports that nine out of 10 Black Canadians, immigrants, and nonimmigrants graduate from high school, and seven out of 10 Canadians go on to achieve a postsecondary diploma (Statistics Canada 2020). Look at that data closely: in Canada, there is no racial disparity between Black, immigrant, and nonimmigrant Canadians when it comes to high school graduation. In America, it's a different story. While nine out of 10 White Americans graduate from high school, the U.S. National Center for Educational Statistics (NCES) reports eight out of 10 Black and Hispanic Americans to finish high school (NCES 2020). This indicates that the racial disparities seen in the United States are due to school systems, programs, and instructional practices, not children themselves. The racial disparity in American high school graduation rates is a significant American problem, as high school dropouts are more likely than graduates to be arrested, have a child while still a teenager (Hernandez 2011), make less money, pay less tax, or wind up in prison. According to *Education Week*, the U.S. high school dropout rate also has profound financial implications for American society as a whole, as every dropout means approximately $260,000 in lost wages, taxes, and productivity (Riley and Peterson 2008). Across North America, high school dropouts are costly for everyone. The American Institutes for Research report, "Insufficient literacy skills exclude far too many children, adolescents, and adults from pursuing their academic, career, and

24

life goals (American Institutes for Research 2020)."

- *Head to college.* A college degree potentially gives humans improved opportunities for jobs, economic stability, higher self-esteem, and greater job satisfaction. Statistics Canada reports zero Canadian racial disparity between Blacks, immigrants, and nonimmigrants receiving a postsecondary diploma or degree (Statistics Canada 2020). American K–12 school systems and postsecondary institutions are getting better at reducing racial disparities in postsecondary completion rates, but American racial disparities continue to exist. Good news: 2015 U.S. Census data reported almost one out of three Americans held a bachelor's degree or higher (Ryan and Bauman 2016). Great news: 2016 U.S. National Center for Education Statistics (NCES) data documented increased postsecondary degree completion rates for Blacks and Hispanics and reductions in racial disparity in postsecondary completion rates between White, Black, and Hispanic Americans. Sadly, American racial disparities continue, as 35% of White Americans receive a college degree compared to 20% of Black Americans and 15% of Hispanic

25

Americans (NCES 2019d). As racial disparities are not evident in postsecondary completion data in similar countries, it is clear that American educational systems and policies need dramatic equity-driven revisions. As Howard University Professor Dr. Ivory Toldson (2019), editor-in-chief of *Journal of Negro Education* and executive editor of *Journal of Policy Analysis and Research,* says, "We don't need to close the Black-White achievement gap; we need to deconstruct it."

- *Find a satisfying job.* In the twenty-first century, literacy skills must go beyond being able to glance through a newspaper or listen to a newscast. Educated global citizens must be able to analyze data, submit complex online forms, identify credible news sources, and think critically to qualify for a job that pays well enough to support themselves and their families. It is challenging to attain a satisfying career when you can't do more than signing your name or complete a simple form.

6. *Literacy has an intergenerational impact.* According to Amy Rea (2020), author of *Library Journal's* "How Serious is America's Literacy Problem?" "Parents who are struggling with literacy are also more likely to struggle with employment and income and, in turn, pass those struggles down to their children." According to Sharon Darling, president and founder of the National Center for Families Learning (NCFL), "These are parents who feel so defeated. Their children start having problems in school, and the parents think, 'That's what happened to me, too'" (Rea 2020).

7. *Literacy predicts life outcomes.* In addition to economic impact, literacy levels also impact health and the likelihood of going to prison.
   • *Health.* According to the Center for Health Care Strategies, 36% of Americans have low health literacy (Mahadevan 2013), which is estimated to cost the U.S. economy up to $236 billion annually (Somers and Mahadevan 2010). When England's National Literacy Trust 2018 scholarly research examined the link between literacy and life expectancy by studying common health and socio-economic factors, researchers found that people with lower literacy levels were

more likely to be unemployed and have low incomes and poor health, and these socio-economic factors were linked to lower life expectancy (Gilbert et al. 2018).

- *Likelihood of incarceration.* People in U.S. prisons are significantly more likely to be illiterate than the general population; the Literacy Project Foundation reported that three out of five people in U.S. prisons couldn't read (Literacy Project Foundation 2017), and 89% of juvenile offenders have trouble reading (Literacy Project Foundation 2017). The American Civil Liberties Union (ACLU), a national nonprofit committed to defending and preserving individual rights and liberties, reports, "(T)he 'school-to-prison pipeline,' (is) a disturbing national trend wherein children are funneled out of public schools and into the juvenile and criminal justice systems. Many of these children have learning disabilities or histories of poverty, abuse, or neglect and would benefit from additional educational and counseling services. Instead, they are isolated, punished, and pushed out (ACLU n.d.)."

Clearly, literacy has a powerful impact on one's life opportunities. The impact on life outcomes must escalate society's urgency to universally improve literacy in schools.

Literacy Around the World

According to the International Literacy Association, 12% of the world's population is either illiterate or functionally illiterate as they lack a basic ability to read (Rea 2020). With 770 million people around the world unable to sufficiently read and write, illiteracy is a massive global problem (Truman Center for National Policy 2013). The international economic implications of illiteracy are staggering. The Truman Center reports, "Illiteracy limits people in developing countries and inner cities, stifles opportunities for innovation, and dampens the economic potential of hundreds of millions. Reading and writing are essential skills for economic mobility. To boost both the U.S. and global economy, we must invest in solutions to promote literacy on a global level (Poff Roman 2010)."

Literacy in America

According to the United States Department of Education, one in five Americans is illiterate (NCES 2019b). That's 43 million Americans who can't read and write sufficiently to analyze information, think critically, and evaluate data to make informed decisions.

U.S. Literacy Rates Are Worse Than in Many Developed Countries. With 43 million Americans unable to read sufficiently to understand and evaluate information, think critically, make informed decisions, and consequently fully participate in society (NCES 2019b), there are more illiterate Americans than the entire population of Canada (Statistics Canada 2016a).

The National Center for Education Statistics (NCES), a branch of the U.S. Department of Education, is the primary federal agency collecting and analyzing data related to education in the United States and other nations. NCES reports, "Nearly two-thirds of fourth graders read below grade level, and the same number graduate from high school still reading below grade level. This puts the United States well behind many other countries in the world, including Japan, all the Scandinavian countries, Canada, the Republic of Korea, and the UK (Rea 2020)." Compared to other developed countries, the United States, the second richest (Wikipedia 2021) and the sixth most well-educated country in the world, is ranked 13th in the world in reading by the International PISA test, failing to achieve the same reading skills as students in China, Estonia, Canada, Ireland, and Poland (Johnson Hess 2018).

American illiteracy rates have a profound impact on both the American economy and the global economy. According to the World Literacy Foundation, America needs to recognize the national and global costs of illiteracy. "The cost of illiteracy to the global economy is estimated at USD $1.19 trillion. The effects of illiteracy [include] . . . limited opportunities for employment or income generation and higher chances of poor health, turning to crime and dependence on social welfare or charity (World Literacy Foundation, n.d.)." For a problem that can be addressed with teachers and books, illiteracy remains remarkably challenging for too many countries, including America.

American literacy rates are impacted by where you live. There is a significant literacy disparity state by state (see Figure 1.1). According to the Organization for Economic Cooperation and Development (OECD), over 17 million Americans are "unable to successfully determine the meaning of sentences, read relatively short texts to locate a single piece of information, or complete simple forms (OECD 2013)." The National Center for Educational Statistics (NCES) reports that there is a significant variance between states regarding the percentage of the population that has below a fifth-grade level of literacy. The highest literacy rates across America are in New Hampshire (94.2%), Minnesota (94%), and North Dakota (93.7%). The lowest literacy rates in America are in Florida (80.3%), New York (77.9%), and California (76.9%) (Rea 2020).

U.S. READING LITERACY
PERCENTAGE OF THE POPULATION OF EACH STATE THAT HAS
BELOW A FIFTH GRADE LEVEL OF LITERACY

Figure 1.1. United States reading literacy by state.

Source: National Center for Education Statistics. National Assessment
of Adult Literacy

American literacy rates vary by race and income.
U.S. literacy rates vary tremendously based on race and
socioeconomic status. As President Barack Obama said in
2009, "The relative decline of American education is
untenable for our economy, unsustainable for our
democracy, and unacceptable for our children, and we
cannot afford for it to continue" (Annie E. Casey Foundation
2010).

**Literacy disparity is a systems problem, not a people
problem.** We know this by comparing U.S. literacy rates to
a similar country. While Canada has a population about one-
tenth the size of America, there are important similarities
between these two wealthy, predominantly white,
predominantly English-speaking countries. Both countries

are among the top 10 richest countries in the world, with the United States being one of the richest and Canada ranking ninth globally (World Population Review 2022). Both are in the top 10 countries in educational expenditures per student, with America spending $14,100 per K–12 students and Canada spending $11,900 per K–12 student (NCES 2017). Politicians in both countries get elected by expressing their value of and commitment to public education. Both countries fund their schools by state versus federally funding, school districts are overseen by locally elected school boards, and while schools are diverse, there is ever-growing diversity by race (NCES 2018; Statistics Canada 2016b).

Overall, the differences between these two public education systems was examined by Canadian Research Chair and former Ontario Deputy Minister of Education Ben Levin, who reported:

> *Canada has consistently been a high-performing country on international assessments of student performance. Compared to the U.S., the main difference is that Canada has a much smaller proportion of low-performing students; performance at the top end of the distribution is quite similar.* (Levin 2011)

If Canada, a smaller-populated country with less wealth and fewer expenditures on education per student, has a smaller proportion of low-performing students, what is different between the two countries? Looking at graduation rates between the two countries by race, Statistics Canada documents that nine out of 10 Black, immigrant, and nonimmigrant Canadians graduate from high school, which shows there is *no* Canadian disparity in literacy rates between White Canadians, and Black Canadians, and Canadian immigrants. By contrast, NCES reports that 9.2 out of 10 White Americans graduate from high school, while 8.5 out of 10 Black Americans and 6.7 out of 10 Hispanic Americans get their high school diploma (NCES 2019d). As reflected by American high school graduation rates, there is a significant American disparity in academic success based on race.

Inequitable American literacy rates and high school graduation rates are intolerable and absolutely reparable by dismantling systemic racism through implementing equity-driven systems, policies, and practices using good data, thoughtful analysis, and compassionate understanding to accomplish equitable, measurable outputs (Toldson 2019).

For over 50 years, U.S. studies have verified that there is a significant gap between American White and Black students' achievement in reading (Hanushek 2016). Fundamentally, American schools do a fine job of teaching reading to White kids, but America's track record for teaching Black and Brown kids is catastrophic. In the U.S. Department of Education's National Center for Educational Statistics (NCES) *The Condition of Education 2020* report, of the 43 million Americans who cannot read, they differentiate the data by race:

- *White.* The largest percentage of the illiterate population are White, native-born Americans. But illiteracy rates are not proportional to the U.S. population; while 76% of the 2019 U.S. population are White (U.S. Census Bureau 2019), only 35% of illiterate Americans are Caucasian, with 94% of them born in the United States.

- *Black.* African Americans make up 13.4% of the U.S. population (U.S. Census Bureau 2019), yet, disproportionately, 23% of adults with low literacy are African American, with 87% born in the United States.

- *Hispanic.* While people of Hispanic or Latino heritage make up 18.5% of the U.S. population (U.S. Census Bureau 2019), 34% of low literacy adults are Hispanic, with 29% native born and 71% non-native born.

In the Twenty-First Century, Why Do American Racial Disparities in Literacy Still Exist?

1. *Follow the Racism.* Caste-based thinking impacts North American society's economy, systems, and policies. According to best-selling author Isabel Wilkerson, America has historically functioned as a caste-based society. (Wilkerson 2020). Her research revealed that ever since Europeans began kidnapping and enslaving Africans in the 1600s, America became a global economic powerhouse on the backs of African laborers brought to the country against their will. Unfortunately, racial atrocities are not unique to America. Canada has its own tragic racial disparities, including but not limited to European settlers stealing land from Indigenous peoples, creating appalling residential schools for Indigenous children, and building the Canadian railway system through the manual labor of Asian immigrants. South Africa suppressed Black citizens through Apartheid throughout most of the twentieth century. *Daily Show* host Trevor Noah, author of *Born a Crime,* reports that racism is "an all-too-common idea or a common theme that happens all around the world" (Hobson 2019). This is systemic racism.

2. *Follow the Money.* Local American school boards determine how much money schools get and how this money is spent. As schools are largely funded by their neighborhoods, white citizens historically elected white school board members who created Eurocentric systems and policies that determined school district size and location and ultimately controlled each school's funding. This is systemic racism.

   Local school funding determines how many teachers a school can have, how many books the school can buy, and whether the building is kept in good repair. This funding system works well in the middle- and upper-class American neighborhoods, as they have a strong tax base and, therefore, well-funded schools. If a school is in a less affluent neighborhood and has been historically underfunded, there is a lot of catching up to do in terms of program funding, resource acquisition, and building maintenance (Joffe-Walt 2020). This is systemic racism.

3. *Follow the Policies.* Since the 1867 Emancipation Proclamation, local American housing policies explicitly and implicitly determined where Black and Brown people could live, limited their economic

prospects, impacted the local tax base, and therefore determined the quality of education in different neighborhoods. In the nineteenth and twentieth centuries, historic "redlining" of neighborhoods, which literally meant drawing red lines on maps that dictated where Black and Brown people could live (Berger 2013), segregated where certain Americans could buy homes, which in turn determined the tax base that impacted school funding (McGhee 2020). The educational and taxation systems in place in American neighborhoods determine the quality of education and therefore impact the literacy rate of every school (Kendi 2019). This is systemic racism.

Twentieth-century Americans were told that there were 'good' neighborhoods and 'bad' neighborhoods, using words like 'urban blight,' 'inner city,' 'high crime,' and 'poverty-stricken areas' were dog-whistles to mask historically racist systems and policies. Best-selling author Ibram X. Kendi says, policies are the problem, not people. "Some people get more, while others get less… because policies don't always grant equal access" (Kendi, 2020). There are no bad neighborhoods, only bad policies. This is systemic racism.

These heartbreaking systemic inequities have been known for years. As documented by the Annie E. Casey

Foundation, the U.S. Department of Education's 2009 National Assessment of Educational Progress (NAEP) reading test concluded that 67% of all Fourth Graders across America were *not* proficient in reading (Annie E. Casey Foundation 2010). When the NAEP reading test was further analyzed:

- 58% of White students were not yet proficient in reading.

- 84% of Black students were not yet proficient in reading.

- 83% of Hispanic students were not yet proficient in reading.

- 83% of children from low-income families were not yet proficient in reading, and 85% of these students attended high-poverty schools.

NAEP reported that performance gaps remained stubbornly wide between lower-income students and their affluent peers (Wexler 2018). This is a systems problem, not a problem with the students themselves. These disparities are due to opportunity gaps rather than achievement gaps. *Street Data* authors Shane Safir and Jamila Dugan (2021) report that inequitable outcomes in American "big picture testing," statewide tests, or "satellite data" are well documented. New York University researcher Jill Gandhi advocates for replacing the term *achievement gap* "... with a term that highlights the root of long-standing disparities in educational resources and access: the opportunity gap" (Gandhi 2021).

Literacy Rates and Dyslexia: In case you think that illiteracy is entirely due to reading disabilities, think again. While reading disabilities present literacy challenges, they do not present insurmountable blockades to becoming critical thinkers, data analysts, effective problem-solvers, or informed voters.

International Dyslexia Association (2016) reports that 5% to 15% of world citizens are impacted by dyslexia. The U.S. Department of Education's National Center for Education Statistics reports that 5.1% of American students receive special education support for specific learning disabilities (NCES 2019a). Approximately 3.5% of American students, or just over 2 million children, receive special education services for a reading disorder (Society for Neuroscience 2004).

Dyslexia requires specially designed instruction to develop differentiated strategies to ensure students can analyze and evaluate information. While dyslexia impacts one's ability to decode and process information, it does not prohibit reading comprehension or critical thinking. Yes, we need to have effective instruction to address dyslexia. But it is racist systems and policies that perpetuate illiteracy, not simply physiological challenges.

Literacy matters. We need to make changes that benefit every kid, as they will grow up to be our future voters and civic leaders. We need them to be well-informed, culturally competent, and ready to work together so we can shift our schools and communities to equity-centered systems that benefit every human. This means a simultaneous grassroots one-child-at-a-time approach synced with a top-down, equity-driven approach. Dismantling systemic racism piece by piece is a huge challenge, but it can absolutely be accomplished by working together in our schools, our local communities, and our global societies.

Next, we need to explore the powerful pivot point of Third Grade to build learning momentum.

Back to My Finest Teachers . . .

Two months into 2020's pandemic-driven springtime remote learning, our school became a well-intentioned mishmash of inadvertently overwhelming and underwhelming families with online activities, nonaligned schedules, and a lack of equitable hardware and Wi-Fi access. As I connected with students and families from my laptop, I felt exhausted, overwhelmed, and adrift, but I was determined to pivot. Meanwhile, my students were impacted in different ways:

- *Kindergarten scientist Malik* was coping. His already-formed habit of reading at home nightly with his parents helped him quickly adjust to the increased levels of reading at home. As his family had well-established positive partnerships with teachers, Malik pivoted to learning at home as well. While he preferred traditional school, his grit and perseverance paid off. With systems in place, he was sustaining his reading momentum.

- *First Grade artist Sophie* was angry and anxious. She felt bereft when her social interactions suddenly ceased. Her mother was frantic and contacted Sophie's teacher and me seeking help with her daughter's big emotional outbursts and refusals to complete her virtual assignments. We collaborated on how to help this struggling child, partnering with Sophie's mom via multiple video calls with both Mom and daughter to get this frantically flummoxed First Grader calmed down, reconnected, and refocused on learning.

- *Third Grade leader Isabella* was lost. Her parents scrambled to deal with their own work issues while also trying to get technology into their daughter's hands. Without reliable technology and social interactions, Isabella was inequitably isolated and wasn't practicing her reading at home. Without her daily confidence-building leadership responsibilities, she was becoming unfocused and disconnected.

Five months into 2020's remote learning, data from an August 2020 school-based family survey at my school showed that 56% of families wanted immediate help to support their child with reading during remote learning. It was time to refine practices to support teachers and parents.

Next Steps

1. *Create a Momentum Journal.* Record your thoughts as you progress through the book. Reflecting can stimulate your momentum as you move forward. (If journaling isn't your thing, then skip it.) Space is provided in every Momentum Checklist to capture your thinking and reflect on your Learning Journey.

2. *Be conscious of Your Own Reading Experiences (YORE).* This is your personal history of the positive and negative experiences you experienced as you learned to read. Reflect on the challenges and

injustices you may have faced at school. If you didn't face learning struggles, acknowledge the privileges you were afforded. Be mindful of your own life history, learning journey, reading experiences, and feelings swirling around your head and your heart. We must face history and ourselves before we can help our learners.

3. *Love Your Finest Teacher(s).* As mentioned at the start of this book, the students I worry about the most are My Finest Teachers because they will teach *me* the most every year. Every single one of My Finest Teachers continues to live in my heart. They are the foundation of my innovations and my own learning. Throughout my career, they taught me how to individualize responses, strengthen relationships, differentiate instructional practices, and create Personalized Empowerment Projects. *As you read this book, keep Your Finest Teacher (YFT) in mind and close to your heart, as their reading needs, struggles, and triumphs will fuel their momentum and yours.*

To keep our work student-centered, each chapter will end with a Momentum Checklist using the same inquiry process we want young readers to follow when critically thinking about a text: *reflect, assess, plan, do.* While these ideas are focused on school-based implementation, families can use them as well.

Chapter 1: Momentum Checklist

Reflect: Reflecting on Your Own Reading Experiences (YORE) will inform your instructional and leadership practices and is a crucial first step to supporting Your Finest Teacher. In your Momentum Journal:

- Record YORE: Were you raised in a family with a strong reading culture, or was your family focused on other areas? Do you remember a favorite book or favorite teacher? What privileges were you afforded? Can you remember learning to read? What were your feelings about reading? If you were successful, how did it feel? If you struggled, how did it feel?

- Identify Your Finest Teacher (YFT) by writing down their name to honor who they are, identifying their strengths in class, on the playground, and in the community, and identifying areas they are working on.[4]

Assess: Assessment helps us determine where we are, where we want to go, and how we plan to get there. Interview, survey, gather data, and/or observe students, as

---

[4] Using Ross Greene's "Assessment of Lagging Skills and Unsolved Problems" can be a helpful tool. https://livesinthebalance.org/wp-content/uploads/2021/06/ALSUP-2020.pdf.

well as survey their parents to: identify strengths; identify interests; identify where they persevere; identify skills you want to target; identify potential elements that are impacting learning (food security, lack of practice, lack of reading stamina, lack of access to books, etc.)

Plan: Identify end goal(s) to target both skills and confidence. Target skills based on end goal(s). Identify timeline, potential challenges, and how you might address the challenges.

Do: Keep reading to identify systems and strategies you can implement as a teacher or school leader to help every child learn to read.

Momentum Checklist

☐ *Reflect*

☐ *Assess*

☐ *Plan*

☐ *Do*

Chapter 2

The Powerful Pivot Point of Third Grade

"The relative decline of American education is untenable for our economy, unsustainable for our democracy, and unacceptable for our children, and we cannot afford to let it continue."

—President Barack Obama

When I think back to my own experiences in Third Grade, I remember learning to read chapter books, struggling with mastering multiplication facts, and wrestling with learning cursive handwriting. My memories include a plethora of reading comprehension worksheets as my classmates and I trudged through the assignments. My mom, a former teacher and my ever-present champion, ignored my complaints and nudged me along my learning path with determination and perseverance. She knew that hard work and struggle were crucial parts of my development. By the time I reached the end of Third Grade, persistence was my superpower. Looking back on my Third Grade Self, I know I need to be acutely mindful of the privilege I was afforded: I did not face intergenerational trauma, poverty, or racism. Bringing one's Own Reading Experiences along is a potent reflection tool to explore the powerful pivot point of Third Grade.

Why Is Third Grade a Fundamental Pivot Point?

Being able to read at grade level by the end of Third Grade is a key predictor of success in life. It takes years to learn to read. While each of us may not remember exactly when we progressed from sounding out "c-a-t" to laughing at Pilkey's *Captain Underpants*, crying at the end of White's *Charlotte's Web*, or curling up with Rowling's Harry Potter series, we indeed shifted from learning to read to reading to learn. Experts explain that Third Grade is the "turning point for this fundamental pivot point (Hernandez 2011).

Reading by the End of Third Grade Predicts Future Success in School: A Third Grader's ability to read at grade level by the end of the school year is an indicator of both their future success in school and their potential to graduate from high school. The National Conference of State Legislators stated in 2019 that "Third Grade has been identified as important to reading literacy because it is the final year children are learning to read, after which students are "reading to learn." If they are not proficient readers when they begin Fourth Grade, as much as half of the curriculum they will be taught will be incomprehensible" (Weyer and

Casares 2019). Annie E. Casey Foundation reported, ". . . millions of American children get to fourth grade without learning to read proficiently. And that puts them on the dropout track."

According to Donald J. Hernandez (2011), author of the study "Double Jeopardy: How Third-Grade Reading Skills and Poverty Influence High School Graduation."

We teach reading for the first three grades, and then after that, children are not so much learning to read but using their reading skills to learn other topics. In that sense, if you haven't succeeded by Third Grade, it's more difficult to [remediate] than it would have been if you started before then. (Hernandez 2011)

When Hernandez analyzed reading scores and later graduation rates of 3,975 students born between 1979 and 1989 in the Bureau of Labor Statistics *1979 National Longitudinal Survey of Youth*, he found that 16% did not graduate from high school by age 19. Historically, students who struggled with reading in an early elementary school comprised 88% of those adults who did not graduate.

Reading by the End of Third Grade Predicts College and Job Prospects: The ability to read by the end of Third Grade impacts the likelihood of graduating from high school, which is an essential stepping-stone to college and getting a good job. In 2020, the American Educational

Research Association (AERA) reported that "a student who can't read on grade level by Third Grade is four times less likely to graduate by age 19 than a child who does read proficiently by that time" (Sparks 2011). AERA goes on to add that if our nonproficient Third Grader is also living in poverty, they are ". . . 13 times less likely to graduate on time than his or her proficient, wealthier peer." Third Grade reading is a key predictor of heading to college and getting a well-paying job.

Third Grade Reading Can Predict Life Outcomes: As a student's ability to read by the end of Third Grade predicts their future success in school, it consequently predicts life outcomes. High school dropouts have an increased risk of getting a low-paying job, living in poverty, having food security issues, going to prison (Richardson and Judge 2013), and having long-term health issues due to poor healthcare. This has a profound impact on the individual and on society. According to the Annie E. Casey Foundation (2010), "The bottom line is that if we don't get dramatically more children on track as proficient readers, the United States will lose a growing and essential proportion of its human capital to poverty, and the price will be paid not only by individual children and families but by the entire country."

It is clear that ensuring students learn to read by the end of Third Grade is essential. This is a tall order, but nothing less will do. There is no magic curriculum or miracle software tool, or special gadget that is going to fix it. But the truth is this: We cannot afford to perpetuate systems that are unfair, especially for those children and families furthest from educational justice. It is essential that our children of today, who will become our voters and workers of tomorrow, are able to think critically about what they are reading to make informed decisions and live their lives responsibly and safely. Being able to read by the end of Third Grade is a key stepping-stone in their future.

Learning from My Finest Teachers . . .

1. *Kindergarten scientist Malik* quickly pivoted to remote learning during the early months of the global pandemic due to his established perseverance and his family's established routines and partnerships with staff. Over the spring and summer of 2020, his family continued to read aloud to him daily and helped him access online books from the public library, which he read on his school-provided device. Once school started in September, Malik's family eagerly helped their soon-to-be First Grader pick up his district laptop to continue fostering his learning and daily Home Reading routines.

2. *First Grade artist Sophie* eventually adjusted to remote learning in Spring 2020, but she resumed her emphatic balking against remote learning in September due to her big feelings at home that centered around social isolation and anxiety. The culmination of a summer lacking in playdates and reading routines resulted in a sad and anxious about-to-be Second Grader. Sophie's mother was able to arrange for a tutor and for full-time childcare so she could continue working, yet Sophie started the school year continuing to ardently resist reading practice.

3. *Third Grade leader Isabella* started remote learning in September 2020 with trepidation and anxiety. Ending the previous school year without dependable technology or her empowering daily leadership opportunities at school with her friends had left her lost in the spring. With a district-provided device in hand in September, she began the school year highly motivated to connect with classmates online but not yet highly motivated to read every day.

Chapter 2: Momentum Checklist

Reflect: Specifically focusing on Third Grade, reflect on Your Own Reading experiences (YORE) in Third Grade. Do a 10-minute write in your Momentum Journal.

- Record YORE for Third Grade, documenting memories and acknowledging strengths, challenges, and privileges.
- Thinking about Your Finest Teacher (YFT), what are the commonalities and differences between your Third Grade experiences and their current reality? How might you use these commonalities and differences to inform how you support YFT?

Assess: Looking at reflections comparing Your Third Grade Reading Experiences and YFT's reading experiences, are there specific formative assessment data points you want to gather throughout the year? Identify individual data points that will help you track YFT's progress (for example, DIBLES[5] or Fountas and Pinnell[6]).

Plan:

- Identify end goal(s) to target both skills and confidence.
- Identify data you will gather and establish a system for data collection that is efficient and effective.
- Build assessment time into your daily schedule. For example, read with YFT regularly during small group instruction and while classmates are in Independent Daily Reading (IDR) time.
- Target skills based on end goal(s). Identify timeline, potential challenges, and how you may address the challenges.

---

[5] DIBLES, or Dynamic Indicator of Basic Literacy Skills, is University of Oregon's tool to assess the acquisition of literacy skills. These assessments are intended to be quick fluency measures designed to identify struggles early, allowing teachers to responsively provide differentiated instruction to meet individual beginning readers' needs. https://dibels.uoregon.edu/.

[6] Fountas and Pinnell (F&P) provide a fluency and reading comprehension tool for benchmarking reading levels in order to ensure that students are provided with text that is "just right" for them so they can read with accuracy and comprehension. https://www.heinemann.com/collection/fp.

Do: Put your plan into action and monitor how it is going. Refine your systems to meet YFT's emerging needs and your needs as you design efficient, equity-centered systems.

Momentum Checklist

☐ *Reflect*

☐ *Assess*

☐ *Plan*

☐ *Do*

The What

"The fire of literacy is created by the sparks between a child, a book, and the person reading. It isn't achieved by the book alone, nor by the child alone, nor by the adult who is reading aloud—it's the relationship winding between all three, bringing them together in easy harmony."

—Mem Fox, children's author, and reading expert

—

As Mem Fox (2008) wisely observed, learning to read is a dynamic process. Chapters 3 through 5 explore:

- Creating and accelerating momentum
- Implementing research-based reading instruction
- Teaching the whole child by infusing social-emotional learning and culturally responsive practices into reading instruction.

Chapter 3

Creating Momentum

"When you find yourself in the thick of pursuing a goal or dream, stop only to rest. Momentum builds success."

—Suzy Kassem, author

Whenever I see students struggling with learning how to read, I remind myself of my experience learning to ride a bike. As a seven-year-old, I begged my parents for a bike so I could join the kids next door who joyfully zoomed around on their bikes with pride and glee. After begging my parents and doing many extra chores, I received my first bike: a beautiful azure blue machine with gleaming fenders and trusty handlebar grips. With visions of newfound independence in my head, I immediately hopped on and attempted to ride it. Unfortunately, I was naïve about the imperative of balance and momentum in bike riding and immediately crashed to the ground, skinning my knee. The fact that this mortifying mishap happened in front of the very neighborhood kids I wanted to join made it all the worse. Defeated, I avoided my beloved blue bike for several weeks until my exasperated mother finally marched me outside, gave me a much-needed pep talk about determination and perseverance, and coached me as I anxiously practiced. After many skinned knees, I finally got the hang of it and joined the other kids with pride. But I conjure up this memory often so that I remember that it takes momentum to help a nonreader move forward to learn to read.

What Is Momentum?

As so well stated in Farshad Asl's (2016) quote, "Momentum is the bridge between vision and results." Momentum is the cognitive and emotional force that drives us to move forward to do something new or daunting. It is the energy that compels us to get off the couch, out the door, and onto the bike for the first time, even when we know, it may be hard. It is important to note that momentum is equal parts head, and heart, as I needed to cognitively develop my bike riding skills to learn *how* to ride a bike and overcome my fears by thinking about *why* I wanted to ride my bike. Momentum is also about starting to move forward and continuing to move forward. How do we help a student to start moving forward and keep moving forward in reading?

First Law of Physics—The Law of Inertia: English mathematician Sir Isaac Newton explained the process of momentum's impact on learning using his First Law of Physics, The Law of Inertia: People tend to do what they are already doing. If your bicycle is stopped, then you stay stopped. If your bicycle is moving forward, then you *keep moving forward* (Summit Academy 2016).

As reading expert Dr. Richard Allington (2011), explains, reading is a complex cognitive process. So, it can be challenging to overcome inertia to get a beginning reader moving forward to make progress. To help a student begin to learn to read, we not only need to ensure they feel belonging and safe in the classroom, but we also need to develop reading skills, collaborate with families to identify student passions, and increase reading practice. These concepts will be addressed in the chapters ahead.

Momentum works the same way for adults—be it the teacher or family members helping children at home. We all need to initiate and sustain our own momentum to try new teaching practices, maintain routines, and adapt our responses to meet the needs of every student. And just like students, educators can get "stuck" in our own behavior patterns sometimes. Moving forward to try new approaches is just as important for adults as it is for kids but shifting from the known to the new is hard! While it is challenging for adults to shift gears to change long-held beliefs and antiquated practices, it is essential to *stop* what isn't working and *pivot* to effective, efficient actions. For teachers, this may be shifting from outdated past practices to research-based, equity-centered instructional methods. For families, this may mean shifting from exasperation with our procrastinating kids to finding new strategies for helping kids to accomplish a task with confidence. Moving forward and sustaining progress takes practice, patience, and persistence for children and adults alike!

Second Law of Physics—Sustaining Momentum: Sir Isaac Newton would be proud of my bike riding persistence. To sustain progress, Newton would tell us that *if it is working, keep doing it!* Practicing riding my bike strengthened my balance, bike riding skills, and confidence. Ongoing practice literally and figuratively sustained my momentum. We need to ensure that we sustain the learning momentum of beginning readers to shift them to confident, skillful readers.

Third Law of Physics—For Every Action, There Is an Equal and Opposite Reaction: Beginning readers start off with a variety of emotions about learning to read. Many are flooded with trepidation, as "in the beginning, they don't believe they can read any kind of book." As First Grade teacher Marjorie Roach (2021) says, "We want them to begin to see themselves as readers." Over time, encouragement, instruction, practice, and skill acquisition increase confidence while decreasing anxiety and avoidance.

Self-confidence, skills, and perseverance are essential "muscles" for building learning momentum. To help beginning readers learn to read, teachers provide: guided reading instruction; phonics instruction; small group reading coaching; independent reading practice.

Confidence "muscles" are further strengthened as each item above weaves together to build and solidify skills. For example, the more students practice reading decodable "just right texts," the more students develop reading skills and confidence. Along with reading practice, the more adults encourage the child's attempts to decode, the more the student will persist. The key is to provide specific encouragement for the child's approximations. When they began talking as babies, parents naturally responded to their child, saying, "Mama go," with "Yes, Mommy is going to work!" When learning to read, students need specific encouragement followed by positive, constructive feedback if necessary. To build internal validation rather than dependency on external feedback, encouragement should be specific and focus on effort and process. For example, instead of saying "Great job!" try "I notice you are working hard to sound out that word!" (Dweck 2017). Encourage them as they track the letters with their eyes and finger, decode and make connections. Giving specific feedback for their approximations builds skills and confidence, which in turn strengthens perseverance.

As primary students build their reading "muscles," they eventually get to a specific point (in my experience, this is midway through Second Grade) when they are able to keep a beginning chapter book "in their head" by remembering the characters and plot as they progress through the book. This familiarity lessens the "cognitive load," just like with learning to ride a bike, and the whole reading process gets easier and more fun with practice. This gives young readers the momentum to enjoy reading a familiar series, laugh at the riddles in a joke book, delve into a nonfiction book on a topic they are excited about, follow a recipe in a cookbook, or get scared when reading a mystery. As *New York Times*, best-selling author Malcolm Gladwell (2002) would say, this is the "tipping point" when readers begin to enjoy the act of reading, as they can make connections with greater ease.

With practice, reading becomes easier. As skills are mastered, there is the less cognitive effort required. Skills build reading confidence, which in turn initiates and accelerates momentum. Just as beginning bike riders get better with practice, *reading gets easier and more fun with increased practice.* As novice bike riders ride faster and farther, *beginning readers persist if they have the skills and confidence to do it.* We start to see our passionate readers gain momentum as they shift from "learning to read" to "reading to learn." Our goal here is to ensure that regardless of the timeline they follow, we aim to have every student able to read confidently by the end of Third Grade. This sets them up for academic success by the beginning of Fourth Grade and beyond!

Sir Isaac Newton discovered that it takes strength or force to move an object forward. Similarly to a moving object, it takes *physical, emotional, and social effort* to learn. Medical experts Inzlicht, Shenhav, and Olivola (2018) explained that based on ". . . models in cognitive psychology, neuroscience, and economics, effort (be it physical or mental) is costly . . . (W)hen given a choice, humans . . . tend to avoid effort. . . . (T)he opposite is also true . . . effort can also add value."

Energy Is Needed to Start and Sustain Momentum

To start and sustain momentum, the energy generated and expended during the reading process is a combination of physical energy, emotional energy, and social energy:

- *Physical energy* is expended when brain cells and synaptic connections are generated as students make connections while reading. This is not a new concept; Canadian neuropsychologist Donald O. Hebb (1949) coined "neurons that fire together wire together." This physical energy, defined as *neuroplasticity*, "is the selective organizing of connections between neurons in our brains." Dr. Hebb used this catchy phrase to explain how every experience, thought, feeling, and sensation triggers thousands of neurons to form a neural network. Repeating this experience triggers the same neurons every time, which is how the brain forms a neural pathway. At the end of a busy day, when you have been thinking hard, your brain may actually feel "full," or it may hurt because thinking requires physiological energy. When students repeatedly practice reading or recall a memory, their neural networks (groups of neurons that fire together) create electrochemical pathways (Bernard 2010). *When a student makes a connection, they are literally building brain cells via synaptic connections.* Over time, these connections become thick, robust road maps that link different quadrants of the brain. This is why primary students may be cranky and exhausted during the first few weeks of school, as it takes a lot of energy to think about new ideas, make new friends, and learn routines!

- *Emotional energy* is needed as students read to feel excitement, frustration, and anger. According to Dr. David Hawkins, ". . . emotions had measurable energy and could either foster or negate actual cell life" (Comaford, 2018). As explained in Dr. Hawkins's groundbreaking work, *Power vs. Force (2013)*, a person's measurable energy level increases as that person experiences more positive emotions. Hawkins found that cells actually died when their energy level dropped below a certain point, which is where the emotions of scorn, hate, anxiety, shame, regret, despair, blame, and humiliation reside.

- *Social energy* is expended as students talk with peers and teachers to process the information they are reading. As they listen to classmates, discuss the text, play letter bingo, and collaborate during the lesson, readers spend energy as they interact in social environments in the presence of peers ("Social Dynamics," 2020). Social energy strengthens relationships with teachers and classmates, which in turn positively impacts learning (Gray et al. 2018).

Generating Learning Momentum

Generating learning momentum physically, emotionally, and socially begins with building belonging and trust through relationships. Belonging and trust are foundational for humans to feel safe enough to take risks in learning. Every student needs a Home–School Team working together to support their unique combination of needs.

What We Feed Will Grow: It is important to focus on behaviors we want to see and ignore behaviors we don't want to see. Without a doubt, this is hard but essential! Throughout the day, we need to be mindful that what we pay attention to reinforces the behavior, and ignoring unwanted behavior can extinguish it. *Focus* author Mike Schmoker (2011) urges educators and families to focus on what is most important, as our clarity and priorities are the keys to helping our learners move forward. Jim Collins (2001), author of *Good to Great*, talks about the crucial aspect of focus. "The real path to greatness . . . (is for) . . . each of us to focus on what is vital—and to eliminate all of the extraneous distractions." Teachers and families need to pay attention to what we want to see and do our best to ignore or redirect what we don't want to see in order to help our beginning readers stay on the path to success.

Mindset Can Be a Privilege: Stanford University psychologist and best-selling author Dr. Carol S. Dweck

(2017) wrote in her book *Mindset,* "In a growth mindset, people believe that their most basic abilities can be developed through *dedication* and *hard work*—brains and talent are just the starting point." Dweck asserted that mindset, whether it is a fixed or a growth mindset, has a huge impact on outcomes. While a fixed, "I can't do it!" mindset negatively impacts skill acquisition, confidence, and learning impetus, Dweck stated that a growth mindset allowed educators and families to motivate students to improve learning and created a love of learning and resiliency that fueled goal achievement. Dweck et al. (2014) refer to the powerful impact of a growth mindset as "academic tenacity," which includes belonging academically and socially, working hard, seeking challenges, and being able to persevere over the long haul.

At the same time, it is essential to recognize and address that a growth mindset can be a privilege. A student furthest from educational justice can have the most powerful growth mindset in the world, but the school system may not support it as effectively as it should. With existing racist barriers, not all students are set up for equitable success. Breaking down the barriers that exist for Black and Brown students to ensure every student feels belonging and has research-based instruction and equity-centered resources is imperative for every human in employing a growth mindset at school.

Moving at the Speed of Trust: All educators must keep in mind that students and families furthest from educational justice may carry intergenerational trauma and injustices with them to school *every day*, so a growth mindset requires a great deal of trust building to cultivate. It is the job of teachers and school administrators to initiate, foster, and sustain trust with each family. As educators, we must work especially hard to earn the trust of marginalized families, as systemic racist practices have generated historical mistrust and apprehension for students and families furthest from educational justice. Trust building is the first equity-driven step in supporting students and families who have been mistreated or ignored in the past, and it begins with a simultaneous one-child-at-a-time and top-down deconstruction of racist systems. As American educator and author Stephen Covey (2005) said, "We can only move at the speed of trust."

Momentum Moves

Over the past 36 years, I've worked with and learned from thousands of children, families, and colleagues. I've pored over professional books seeking wisdom and guidance, been inspired by conference presentations and podcasts, collaborated with brilliant colleagues, and worked with children to find a "just right" fit. Over time, I found that reading improved when I consistently implemented the following three strategies.

Three Key Momentum Moves:

1. *Belonging-centered learning.* Interpersonal connections and motivation drive learning (Gray et al., 2018). When kids come to school every day looking forward to seeing *you,* excited to learn about things they are passionate about, and energized by opportunities to work on things they are curious about, learning improves. Fundamentally, learning momentum increases when instruction incorporates students' passions and interests into the classroom and the school day.

2. *Collaborative partnerships.* Learning improves when teachers and families work together. As partnering with your colleagues and your student's families will make you a more effective teacher and leader, we need equity-driven systems, strategies, and tools for effectively and efficiently collaborating with colleagues. And let's face it—it saves time and provides professional joy to collaborate with colleagues and families.

3. *Small moves create big results.* Increasing practice builds momentum and improves reading. Regular independent reading practice with "just right" text accessed inside and outside of the classroom builds motivation to learn to read and strengthens reading skills and confidence.

Creating and Accelerating Momentum

Implementing these three Momentum Moves has a powerful impact on a student's self-concept, confidence, and, ultimately, on learning.

> To create and accelerate momentum, build belonging and trust, establish collaborative partnerships with colleagues and families, and increase practice through passion-centered learning and personalized empowerment projects.

Any one of these factors will work on its own, but combining them magnifies the potential for further acceleration. Examining them in detail will build implementation momentum.

The Power of Belonging-Centered Learning: Belonging is created when humans feel a relationship–a connection to others. When children and adults feel belonging, they feel welcomed, accepted, and loved. When students feel belonging in their classroom, they trust their teacher and feel safe with and accepted by their peers, which motivates them to try new things, take learning risks, and, ultimately, master new concepts and skills.

It is the teacher's responsibility to help every student feel this sort of belongingness in the classroom. This essential feat is accomplished through multiple initiatives, strategies, and approaches, but *it always starts with building interpersonal relationships with students and families.* In addition to relationship building, teachers must establish clear expectations, routines, and a visible schedule so that all students can rely on its predictability and feel safe. Throughout the year, teachers need to explicitly teach social communication skills, problem-solving skills, conflict resolution skills, and the importance of making mistakes. When school leaders and staff work hard to establish a welcoming environment for families, then families, as well as students, build trust with the school. If a student's family trusts the teacher, students are more likely to trust the teacher. As teachers focus on culturally responsive teaching and social justice initiatives with students and families, they strengthen relationships as they help all students honor and learn from cultures all over the world. See Chapter 11 for ideas.

Gray, Hope, and Matthews (2018) identified three types of belongingness or "opportunity structures" that either foster or thwart a student's need to belong.

- *Interpersonal belonging* focuses on relationships and connections between teacher-student, student-student, and home–school.
- *Instructional belonging* develops student engagement in lessons by incorporating and celebrating a student's cultural heritage to strengthen connections and deepen understanding (Gray et al. 2018).
- *Institutional belonging* fosters student engagement and nurtures student motivation by teachers and school leaders integrating culturally responsive teaching practices and eliminating structural barriers at the school level that devalue minoritized populations by providing impactful institutional opportunity structures for students (Gray et al. 2018).

The Power of Collaborative Partnerships: Partnerships support and accelerate student learning. *Professional partnerships* among teachers and administrators create collaborative professional energy that can spur educators to implement research-based innovative teaching practices. *Home–school partnerships* with teachers and parents accelerate learning momentum, as parents literally bring their expertise about their child to the learning table to help staff identify a student's strengths and interests and partner with teachers to foster momentum with encouragement, practice, and support.

The Power of Practice: Practice is essential for learning. Famously investigated in his best-selling book, *Outliers,* author Malcolm Gladwell (2008) asserted that what made musicians, athletes, and business leaders successful was practice more than talent. Gladwell's book was based on the concept of a study showing that successful musicians in an orchestra had practiced 10,000 hours by the time they were 20 years old (Ericsson et al. 1993). To foster and strengthen reading skills and confidence, scheduling regular independent reading practice opportunities throughout the day is essential.

At the same time, humans understandably like to do things we are good at and may avoid things we aren't good at. So, good readers get better, and struggling readers may avoid reading, which results in a lack of skill development and confidence. Having strategies for pairing something we like to do with something we don't like to do helps humans develop new positive habits or refine existing habits. As *Atomic Habits* author James Clear (2018) notes, applying success in one area to success in another area is an effective way to reinforce a habit. Increasing practice takes planning and persistence.

Together, the Three Momentum Moves build and accelerate learning momentum. As Scottish singer-songwriter Annie Lennox says, "When you're that successful, things have a momentum, and at a certain point, you can't really tell whether you have created the momentum or it's creating you."

Learning from My Finest Teachers…

Multilingual Third Grader Isabella was stuck. While she had received extra reading support as well as *English-language learner* (ELL) services throughout First through Third Grade, the extra services were not enough. She was still below grade level in reading at the start of Third Grade. As the family reported that Home Reading wasn't working for Isabella, teachers shifted the focus toward striving to increase the quality and quantity of Isabella's daily reading practice time during Independent Reading Time (IDR) at school. Sadly, Isabella had become a skilled procrastinator and reading avoider during IDR. After observing her, teachers tried to determine "the belief behind the behavior," and they guessed that Isabella felt frustrated, anxious, and self-conscious about her own reading (Adler, 1927). Her avoidance was a direct result of her lack of confidence in reading, which resulted in off-task dramas, and distractions during IDR. Teachers checked in with Isabella and with her family and confirmed their suspicions. We needed to shift Isabella from inertia to momentum, and then we needed to accelerate her momentum.

In her Third Grade year, three Momentum Moves were put in place:

1. *Focus on belonging-centered learning.* Thanks to her long-standing family ties to the school, Isabella had strong interpersonal belonging with teachers, peers, and within the school community. Social communication and relationship skills were two of her superpowers. Throughout the day, her teacher provided specific verbal encouragement rather than general praise, as this strengthened the teacher-student connection for Isabella. We continued Tier II extra reading support services focused on phonics, language skills, and practice while explicitly recognizing and celebrating when Isabella was helpful on the playground and helpful in a class by starting independent reading right away.

   As Isabella's passion was leadership, we increased her daily opportunities to help peers and younger students. We created a Big Buddy Reading Program, so Isabella had a Kindergarten buddy that she read with weekly, and we had a Fifth Grader read with Isabella weekly as her Big Buddy. We created a confidence-building leadership opportunity for Isabella by inviting her to become a Student Playground Coach to build her peer connections and confidence. As we scheduled Student Playground Coach time right before IDR, Isabella arrived in class feeling confident, so she started IDR immediately, which helped her strengthen her identity as a reader. We invited Isabella to present at an assembly about Hispanic Heritage Month to share how her family celebrated their heritage, with her proud parents in attendance. All of these small moves had big results, as Isabella felt interpersonal and instructional belonging, which impacted her reading confidence.

2. *Focus on collaborative partnerships.* To refine our practices with Isabella and her classmates, teachers collaborated through professional development and Professional Learning Networks (PLN) [focused on research-based reading instruction. In addition to our Multi-Tiered Systems of Support (MTSS) meetings to review data and plan student supports, staff and I created after-school collaborative meetings so classroom teachers could partner with a Tier II Reading Specialist and Special Education staff to

gather ideas that would help Isabella and classmates academically, emotionally, and socially.

Teachers and family partnered to refine initial strategies and increase Isabella's practice time at school. During parent-teacher conferences, her parents shared how important Isabella's Hispanic culture was to her, so we purchased culturally responsive "just right" books at her level that focused on Hispanic heritage and purchased more culturally responsive books for the library. While Isabella had balked at reading at home to her family, her parents asked for regular updates on her reading progress so they could cheer on their daughter and celebrate each small step. And knowing how much Isabella loved to share about her culture with others, her parents helped Isabella prepare a presentation for our school's weekly assembly to share how her family celebrated Hispanic Heritage Month. Partnering with family accelerated Isabella's learning momentum.

3. *Focus on increasing practice.* To improve Isabella's reading skills and increase her confidence, *we shifted our practice* to sidestep Isabella's reading procrastination. Increasing her time on task with "just right" books was key. When Isabella's parents reported that Home Reading had become a nightly

battleground, we scheduled extra IDR time with a Big Buddy in Fifth Grade and arranged for Isabella's class to be Big Buddies with Kindergartners. We focused on increasing Isabella's time on task with reading "just right" books during IDR by looking for approximations of expected behavior; putting "just right" books in Isabella's Book Box to eliminate procrastination for book selections; coaching Isabella on starting IDR right away; creating a small coaching moment as soon as Isabella had a book in her hand to whisper how helpful it was when Isabella started right away as this set a great example for classmates.

Extra practice improved Isabella's confidence, strengthened her skills, and accelerated her momentum. When the family was given regular reading progress updates, her parents focused on being Isabella's cheerleaders at home and consistently celebrated each small step in Isabella's reading progress. As her learning passion and persistence were strengthened, Isabella's skills and confidence fueled her reading momentum (Duckworth 2016).

After continuing, extra reading support *and* implementing Three Momentum Moves, Isabella's end-of-year individual reading assessment con-firmed that she was able to read at the end of Third Grade reading level by June. Combining all the Momentum initiatives helped Isabella make over one year's growth by the end of Third Grade. With her academic trajectory changed, these initiatives had a profound impact on Isabella's identity, reading skills, and confidence, which indeed helped her maintain and accelerate her learning momentum.

Chapter 3: Momentum Checklist

Reflect: Focusing on Your Finest Teacher (YFT), do a 10-minute write in your Momentum Journal.

- Record YFT's strengths and interests, as knowing passions and superpowers will help them.
- What is working for YFT? When are they focused and/or productive? What isn't working? Pairing a successful habit with a new habit helps.
- What Three Momentum Moves may help?

Assess:

- After identifying YFT from specific data points (for example, DIBLES or Fountas and Pinnell), create a regular tracking system for monitoring reading progress using running records.
- Schedule time for listening to one or two students every day during IDR. (It takes approximately 6–8 weeks to *teach* primary students how to read independently during IDR and then build their reading stamina so that they are able to read independently). Once this routine is well established in your class (for example, about mid-October), then begin your system of reading

with a few students each day to monitor their progress to monitor "just right" levels and track progress. (This also alleviates the assessment crunch at report card time!)

Plan:

- Identify end goal(s) to target both skills and confidence.
- Identify data you will gather and establish an efficient system for data collection.
- Plan the Three Momentum Moves you will use.
- Plan how you will use strengths, passions, and superpowers to leverage momentum.

Do: Put your plan into action and monitor how it is going. Refine your systems to meet YFT's emerging needs and your needs as you design efficient, equity-centered systems.

Momentum Checklist

☐ *Reflect*

☐ *Assess*

☐ *Plan*

☐ *Do*

Chapter 4

How Do Kids *Actually* Learn How to Read?

"If you are going to get anywhere in life, you have to read a lot of books."

—Roald Dahl, author of *Charlie and the Chocolate Factory and Fantastic Mr. Fox*

I have no idea how I learned to read. While I vaguely recall phonics worksheets and pre-primer readers, I don't remember any of the nitty-gritty details—or struggling. What I do vividly remember is my Mom gifting me Holly Beth Walker's *Meg Duncan and the Disappearing Diamonds* when I finished Second Grade. I remember my gleeful anticipation as intrepid Meg fearlessly solved the mystery. I became hooked on devouring mysteries and thrillers. Finding this hook for each child became my quest as an educator because I know that once we can find a child's passion, we can get them on the learning-to-read journey.

Learning to read is one of the most cognitively complex processes known to humankind (Wigfield et al., 2016). Understanding how these process works are essential for helping our beginning readers develop the cognitive skills they need to become readers.

Four Things You Need to Know Before We Begin:

1. *Learning to read is a complex cognitive process.* Scientists and educators continue to analyze exactly how typical readers translate squiggles on a page into images in their brains to connections in their minds. Readers' neurons are "wired together," so they "fire together" to build established neural pathways to create and accelerate efficient cognitive reading routines. Eventually, beginning readers progress from methodical decoding and recognizing sight words to thinking critically about *what* they are reading and *why* they are reading it.

2. *Learning to read is a unique process for each student.* There is no "one size fits all" series of steps. Typically, most First Graders learn to read in a sequential process incorporating phonics, tracking, building fluency using decodable books, and comprehension. About 25% of students need more reading practice than others (Allington 2011), and within this 25%, 5%to 15% of readers need more intense support in the form of specially designed

instruction (International Dyslexia Association 2016). How much practice and support depend on the needs of each child.

3. *Learning to read does not follow an identical timeline for every learner.* Children learn to read when they are ready physically, emotionally, and socially. Physically, children must have their basic needs met. A child who is hungry, tired, or thirsty isn't going to be ready to function effectively, let alone read. Hence, the essential need to ensure children with food security issues get their needs met with breakfast and lunch programs (Maslow 1943). Beginning readers must also be physically capable of focusing and tracking the letters with their eyes. Emotionally, learners must feel safe and belong to be ready to learn (Gray et al. 2018). This timeline is impacted by the life journey the child, their family, and their ancestors had thus far, as anxiety, poverty, trauma, and intergenerational trauma have a profound impact on reading readiness. Socially, Gray's research clearly shows that ". . . educators who actively facilitate social ties in instructional contexts contribute to an interpersonal opportunity structure . . . or connections between students and teachers." As Gray enthusiastically stated, "Being connected is

important, and service is the name of the game. That's the secret sauce!" (Gray 2021).

4. *Motivation to read impacts reading achievement.* To foster and accelerate a learner's motivation, research clearly shows that teachers must help students to fit in and shine based on student strengths, passions, and superpowers. To help students feel belonging, teachers must foster connections between teachers and students and between students. To foster belonging between teacher and student, the teacher needs to identify and celebrate each student's strengths, interests, and superpowers. Teachers also need to consider an important truth shared by teacher coach Leslie Plettner: *"No one can learn from you if you think that they suck"* (Aguilar and Cohen 2022). Gray's 2018 research indicates that students strive to stand out at their school and fit in with their peers, which he calls the *SOFI framework.* Further, his research suggests that students of color are much less likely to have both needs met (Gray 2018). Teachers must ensure that students feel belonging to establish a solid foundation for their motivation to learn, which sustains and accelerates their learning momentum.

Mapping the "Learning to Read" Journey

From the day a child is born, they are immersed in the language. Families are their child's first teachers. Parental encouragement of each clumsy verbal approximation is essential for language development. When a baby says "ba" while pointing at the ball, their parents enthusiastically exclaim, "Yes! That's a ball! Go get the ball!" As families talk with children, tell stories, read aloud to them, sing songs, involve them in the family's cultural practices and celebrations, listen to audiobooks, and make trips to the library, families are building the foundation for their child's learning to read journey.

As children start school, they bring their language skills and literacy concepts with them. Families continue their role as original teachers and essential cheering squads at home. During the school day, students listen to teachers read stories aloud, "read" their daily Board Message, share Big Books, laugh at joke books, and sing songs with enthusiasm—and then head home to share with their family what they've learned, discovered, struggled with, and accomplished. Classroom libraries and school libraries become new places to explore, while families continue to visit the public library. Multilingual learners arrive with their own foundation of language, and they then scaffold their English language learning to their established understandings. Home–school partnerships are essential, as language development and literacy go hand in hand.

So how do we actually teach a human to learn how to read? When I think about *teaching* a child to read, I think of my husband making salsa verde. Ever the passionate cook, once he's made a dish for the first time, he finesses the recipe over time. With this traditional Mexican sauce, he observes, tastes, and smells his dish to balance its heat, flavors, and nuances. He adapts his recipe based on the availability of seasonal vegetables. He's learned that creative spicing and slowly cooking his spicy concoction brings out the flavors consistently. While no two batches are identical, he sets out to create each batch based on the knowledge he has gleaned over time.

Similarly, a teacher has a tried-and-true, research-based, sequential curriculum and plan in mind to help students achieve state learning standards in reading, but the reading instruction must be differentiated to meet each student's academic, emotional, social, and cultural needs. Instead of making one batch of spicy salsa verde, every primary teacher is simultaneously creating multiple dishes of salsa verde, as well as boeuf bourguignon, fried chicken, chana masala, chow mein, paella, pad thai, sweet potato pie, and a soufflé for dessert. Every day. And they may not see the results for years. Fundamentally, this is why teaching is one of the most challenging and rewarding jobs in the world!

As educational researcher Jean Chall identified, the shift from "learning to read" at the end of Third Grade to "reading to learn" at the start of Fourth Grade should be seen as a process focused rather than binary, as her work affirms the generally accepted notion that students need to have mastered the discrete skills of "learning to read" to transition to the "reading to learn" skills required to comprehend increasingly complex text in middle and high school (Houck and Ross 2012). Chall's model is used here to illustrate the importance of shifting from beginning-to-read skills to skillfully focusing on comprehension and critical thinking. Basically, students need to be able to ride the bike up a hill before they can begin to ride up the mountain range ahead.

For young readers, learning to read is very much like learning to ride a bike. Reading and bike riding are both complex physiological processes involving multifaceted skills developed through intentional practice that must all come together for it to work.

The Learning to Read Hill: Between Kindergarten and Third Grade, beginning readers ascend the Learning to Read Hill (Figure 4.1).

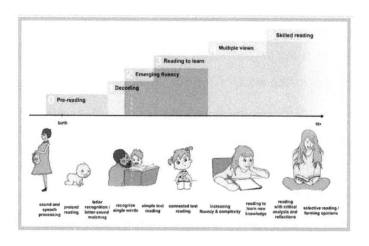

Figure 4.1 The Learning to Read Hill.

Source: Nora Raschle, Réka Borbás, Carolyn King, and Nadine Gaab..
2020. "The Magical Art of Magnetic Resonance Imaging to Study the
Reading Brain." Frontiers for Young Minds.
https://kids.frontiersin.org/articles/10.3389/frym.2020.00072.

Just as beginning riders are motivated to ride by watching others, the complex process of learning to read begins with immersing students in engaging books, from listening to read-aloud to singing songs, hearing oral stories, and watching books on video.

Just as beginning bike riders build momentum by learning to pedal, balance, steer, and brake, beginning readers, synthesize letter names and sounds, phonological rules, and sight words and make connections in their brain in order to get up the Learning to Read Hill.

Just as beginning bike riders need lots of encouragement to get back up when they fall down, beginning readers are empowered by adult encouragement throughout the reading process, so they recognize that they are getting up the Learning to Read Hill!

While beginning bike riders fall down a lot at first, eventually, they learn to put it all together with practice and perseverance. Novice bike riders must increase momentum to ride uphill just as beginning readers build reading momentum by learning to combine sight words and phonological awareness to make connections. *Readers learn to transform the squiggles on the page into symbols in their brains to connections in their minds.* By the end of Third Grade, teachers and families strive to help readers get to the place where they have the momentum to sail downhill with the same joy as an experienced bike rider, ready to shift from learning to read to reading to learning in the years ahead.

The Reading to Learn Mountains: Between the Fourth and Twelfth Grade, readers climb the Reading to Learn Mountains (Figure 4.2). They shift from discrete "learning to read" skills such as decoding to "reading to learn" as they use increasingly complex text for their research and critical thinking. When reading empowers older students to make connections, they further develop their critical thinking skills, questioning skills, communications skills, and creativity (Fullan and Scott 2014). Just like bike riding, the

94

purpose of reading for students is both about the journey and the destination.

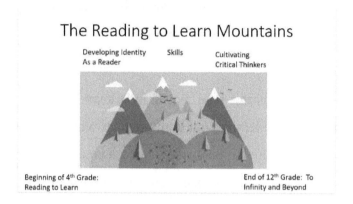

The Reading to Learn Mountains

Developing Identity   Skills   Cultivating
As a Reader   Critical Thinkers

Beginning of 4th Grade: End of 12th Grade: To
Reading to Learn   Infinity and Beyond

Figure 4.2 The Reading to Learn Mountains.

Fundamental Elements of the Reading Process

The learning to read journey is a combination of *immersion* in literacy and *practice*, including the following:

- Rich, culturally responsive literary experiences
- Guided reading instruction
- Read-aloud
- Phonics and phonological instruction
- Sight words
- Independent practice

Let's take a deep dive into each element of the reading process.

Rich literature is well-written, well-designed, engaging fiction and nonfiction that promotes critical thinking, reflection, and perspective-taking, as well as understanding and empathy. Different than decodable books like *Bob Books* or predictable books like *This is the House that Jack Built* and *Fun with Dick and Jane,* rich literature includes beautiful picture books and novels, audiobooks, podcasts, songs, nursery rhymes, chants, online books, and videos. An example is Nyong'o's *Sulwe.*

Culturally responsive is ". . . the ability to learn from and relate respectfully with people of your own culture as well as those from other cultures" (Latino Family Literacy Project, n.d.) Teacher educator and author Zaretta Hammond (2015) examined this crucial concept in her book, *Culturally Responsive Teaching and the Brain,* and created her "Levels of Culture Tree" model to examine culturally responsive teaching through the lens of neuroscience:

A tree is a part of a bigger ecosystem that shapes and impacts its growth and development. Shallow culture is represented in the trunk and branches of the tree, while we can think of surface culture as the observable fruit that the tree bears. Surface and shallow cultures are not static; they change and shift over time as social groups move around and ethnic groups intermarry, resulting in a cultural mosaic just as the branches and fruit on a tree

96

change in response to the seasons and its environment. Deep culture is like the root system of a tree. It is what grounds the individual and nourishes his mental health. (Hammond 2015)

Books from a variety of cultures in different settings are essential components of read-aloud, guided reading lessons and classroom libraries. All children must explore books from a variety of perspectives to develop their understanding and appreciation of many cultures and customs. As Seattle Public Schools Family Partnership Manager Anita Koyier-Mwamba (2020) says, "All children need to read real American stories. They need to be surrounded by literature showing all kinds of families in all kinds of settings."

Gray's research found that recognizing students' various backgrounds was an impactful way to foster motivation (Gray et al 2018). Studies show that culturally responsive texts are especially important for students of color, who have traditionally not seen themselves in books in their white-centric American classrooms (Kromer 2017). Children of color need to see themselves and other Black and Brown kids in the stories they read, and white kids need to see that they are not the only kids living in the world. Moreover, all children need voice and choice in their book selections, so classroom libraries must be well-stocked with texts that open minds and broaden horizons.

Literary experiences reference the importance of literary immersion for all learners, both beginning readers, and lifelong learners. Immersion is key. If a child was in immersion in a foreign language, we would expect that they would listen to the new language being spoken by fluent speakers, speak in this language, listen to stories in this language, and sing songs in this language. All children need to be immersed in a variety of culturally responsive books in class and school libraries so they can see themselves and others in the literary worlds they explore. Just as training wheels help beginning bike riders, early literary experiences form a solid foundation and enhance phonological sensitivity, which empowers our beginning readers up the Learning to Read Hill. Hopefully, this immersive process begins at birth, is supported by family and friends, and continues as young learners first set foot in school. Hopefully, it continues for a lifetime.

Getting up the Learning to Read Hill through Guided Reading Instruction

Research indicates that there are essential components of an effective reading instructional program. This process, called *guided reading instruction* or *balanced literacy*, is an umbrella term for how teachers actually "teach" reading. It includes explicit, research-based reading instruction, read-alouds, phonics, phonological awareness, vocabulary development, and Independent Reading Time.

Explicit, research-based reading instruction with the whole class, small groups, and individual students in phonemic awareness and phonics, decoding, reading comprehension, building vocabulary, and fluency. *Catching Readers Before They Fall* authors Johnson and Keier (2010) found that it is teachers' skillful scaffolding of each aspect of balanced literacy that helps struggling students become confident readers. Just as experienced cooks slowly combine and lovingly cook their salsa verde ingredients over low heat, teachers nurture each learner's development of strategies for processing new texts that become increasingly difficult. Guided reading instruction involves integrating phonemic awareness, decoding, and comprehension altogether. This integration happens when beginning readers daily practice with decodable "just right" text (Scarborough 2001). Each student goes through this process in their own unique way, following a fairly predictable timeline from Kindergarten to the end of Third Grade. Just as practice and determination help beginning bike riders learn to balance while wobbling forward on their bike, beginning readers gradually amalgamate their developing reading skills.

Read-alouds: No matter what their age, learners regularly need to hear thought-provoking literature read aloud! Read-aloud is typically "harder" than the books the child can read themselves, as *beginning readers' listening comprehension is typically two years ahead of beginning readers' actual reading comprehension.* While a child may slowly sound out "The cat sat on the mat," primary readers can absolutely revel in the adventures of Charlotte, the spider in E.B. White's *Charlotte's Web.* As we motivate beginning bike riders to develop their skills in order to ride to the desired destination, read-aloud becomes a highly motivating vehicle for promoting books they will be able to read in the future. It is essential that adults read aloud to children regularly to build a love of literature and ensure that their listening comprehension continues to grow and thrive.

Phonics and phonological awareness: Children learn how to print their own names, and they learn letter names and sounds. They practice, practice, practice blending these letters into words. (c-a-t, b-a-t, br-a-t, fl-a-t). There are 37-word *families* like "at," "it," and "op" to build on, so if a student knows "at," then they can read "cat," "sat," "mat," "rat," "flat," and so on. As author and educational researcher Zaretta Hammond (2015) says, it isn't about "practice makes perfect" but rather "practice makes permanent." She stated:

> *The old adage we usually hear is that "practice makes perfect." Based on what we know about neuroplasticity and deliberate practice, we should rephrase that to read, "practice makes permanent." As you organize yourself for this*

self-reflective prep work, remember that it is not about being perfect but about creating new neural pathways that shift your default cultural programming as you grow in awareness and skill. (Hammond 2015)

Beginning readers need explicit phonics instruction as well as extensive practice with decodable books, word families, letter patterns, and shared reading as they simultaneously develop and integrate phonological awareness, word recognition, and language comprehension in order to be skilled readers (Scarborough 2001).

Vocabulary development ensures sight words are explicitly taught, so children easily recognize the words we see most frequently, such as "the," "on," and "in." Sight words are frequent words we want beginning readers to memorize quickly, as instantly recognizing "the," "them," and "when" simplifies their cognitive load. You can ensure students master basic sight words by having them practice established sight word lists such as Frye or Dolch as part of their English Language Arts (ELA) program.

Independent practice with beginning-to-read books establishes the cognitive connections children need to link letters with meaning, which leads to understanding. Beginning readers progress from decoding single words on a page ("cat," "dog," "lid") to deciphering phrases on a page ("The cat," "the dog," "The lid"), moving to crack simple sentences ("The cat sat" to "The cat sat on the mat."), and eventually, they are ready to decode one to two sentences per page. Scarborough's (2001) research found that skilled reading occurred when independent reading practice began with decodable books, and once short and long vowels were mastered, then readers progressed to practice with predictable text.

Independent practice is an essential facet of getting up the Learning to Read Hill. Every day, beginning readers need to practice with all three of the types of text discussed below.

Reading Levels: Matching Readers with the Right Book for the Right Moment

Just as bike riders need the right-sized bike to be successful, so do beginning readers need an appropriate text based on their reading skills and needs. Just as a too big or too small bike won't help beginning bike riders learn to ride efficiently, similarly, teachers need to get the right books into students' hands based on their learning needs. Understanding the right book for the right moment is essential to help children during instruction and Independent Reading Time.

1. *Instructional reading texts* are books that teachers use during direct instruction to explicitly teach children decoding, comprehension, and critical

thinking skills. These are books that the student can read with 90% accuracy. Teachers use instructional reading texts for whole class instruction and small group work, as students can read most of the words in the book but benefit from the teacher guiding them with both decoding some tricky words and comprehending the concepts. With guidance, students shift from reading these texts with support to being able to read the text independently.

2. *"Just right" books for independent reading* are slightly easier books that beginning readers are able to read on their own. These are books that children can read with 95% accuracy. Beginning readers may have practiced these books in their small group and then confidently read them during Independent Reading Time (IDR). They are not too hard or too easy (Scarborough 2001). Once beginning readers can efficiently and effectively decode short and long vowels, then they shift to predictable text (Allington 2011). As children progress to reading increasingly complex text, primary teachers conduct frequent "running record" reading assessments to ensure books continue to be "just right."

3. *Dessert books* are high-interest books that may be too hard for beginning readers to read on their own, but they love to look through and/or have an adult

read to them. As student agency is a key facet of learning to read, dessert books are equally as important as "just right" texts. High-interest books are key motivational tools to read *after* students work hard to decode their "just right" books. Just like beginning bike riders need to imagine the phenomenal places they will go, so too do beginning readers need to look through books they are excited about. Dessert books are galvanizing and empowering as they drive children to continue up the Learning to Read Hill.

When selecting text to read with beginning readers, Teacher-Mountain-Guides select books based on student reading levels. In small reading groups with a teacher, students read books at their instructional reading level to develop skills and comprehension. When students can confidently read specific books, then these books are now at their independent reading level, and the teacher tucks these "just right" books into their book box as IDR books and/or Home Reading books. Finally, when students have read their "just right" books, they can dive into their dessert books, as their passion-focused books galvanize their momentum up the Learning to Read Hill.

Timeline for Accelerating up
the Learning to Read Hill

Kindergarten children are immersed in the language through listening to oral stories, read-aloud, rhymes, games, and songs. They learn the alphabet letters and the sound(s) each letter makes. Children also learn how to name their feelings, how to stay calm when feeling anxious or angry, and how to get along with classmates. They are beginning to read books with a few words per page or even ones with an entire sentence. Their brain cells are multiplying, their belongingness is (hopefully) increasing to impact their burgeoning skills and confidence, and they are making friends. For both bike riding and learning to read, continuing momentum through practice is key! By the end of Kindergarten, most students are on their way to continue ascending the Learning to Read Hill and developing their love of learning.

By the end of First Grade, learners are able to independently sound out and comprehend two to three sentences per page. Their sight word vocabulary has grown, so they can readily recognize many basic words. As momentum builds, this is the point when the new bike rider shifts from wobbling to balancing with more confidence. Just as there are a lot of skinned knees for beginning bike riders, there are also struggles and frustrations for our beginning readers. By the end of the year, students are aiming to decode "just right" text to try to read dessert books like Keats's *The Snowy Day*. Lots of repetition and encouragement allow beginning readers to get the flow of reading and consequently build their confidence.

Second Graders continue their literary immersion experience by reading stories with lots of familiar characters and simple plots. Approximately midway through Second Grade, as primary readers are able to comprehend increasingly complex texts such as ongoing series with familiar characters like *Frog and Toad are Friends* and *Lola Levine,* young readers are ready to transition to self-selecting books based on their skills and interests. A good rule of thumb for finding a "just right" text for primary and intermediate students is that if they can read the description on the back of the book while only making one or two stumbles, skips, or errors, then the book is at their independent reading level. They may tell you it is too easy at first. Tell them practice builds connections in their brain!

Stories with ongoing, familiar characters, plotlines, and writing styles, like *Elephant and Pig* and *Nate the Great*, allow young readers to learn to hold characters, plots, and their own connections in their head as they finish these longer books over several days. This is where the reader shifts from reading the same picture book over and over to reading a familiar series.

Helping Second Graders find a series or a favorite author is essential, as once elementary readers are interested in a specific series, this becomes a pivotal moment. This is when beginning readers shift into high gear and hopefully get on the path to becoming lifelong readers. Choosing books that they are interested in fosters their positive emotions around reading. Young readers' momentum increases as they enthusiastically devour a favorite series or author. As they talk with classmates about their favorite books during activities like Book Share,*[7] students strengthen confidence and peer connections. Reading now aligns with Vygotsky's all-important social elements, which increase belongingness, engagement, and joy (Johnson and Keier 2010). This is the moment when teachers, school librarians, and families can celebrate success by getting the books students to want to read into their hands.

Third Graders build skills that help them develop confidence as connectors and critical thinkers. Confident readers are increasingly able to self-select books that they can understand. "Not quite there yet" readers need ongoing adult help to continue to select "just right" books for their independent reading, as well as dessert books. Third Grade teachers need to balance a "not quite there yet" student's

---

[7] Book Share is a time when students share the book they are reading with a classmate. It is a way of building connections between peers, promoting books, and continuing to foster a love of books.

skills with their belongingness, autonomy, and interests. Help for "not quite there yet" Third Grade readers include frequent running records by vigilant teachers to ensure that "just right" books are selected instead of "saving face" books that are too hard.

Third Grade is when social interactions can accelerate reading momentum, as talking about favorite books like Cleary's *Runaway Ralph* or Kinney's *Diary of a Wimpy Kid* or thought-provoking novels like Alexander's *The Crossover* can be unifying vehicles for building friendships as well as comprehension. It doesn't matter if children want to read *The Adventures of Captain Underpants* or comics or graphic novels at this point; so long as they are reading books at their independent level, it is our job as adults to encourage and support them! Students will want to read more if their voice and choice selections are aligned with their reading levels, as this accelerates their learning momentum.

In **Fourth through Fifth Grade**, intermediate students are able to understand increasingly complex text. As Third to Sixth Graders transition to the "junior" youth reading level, they can grasp increasingly complex concepts as they build their ability to think critically, problem solve and empathize with characters in diverse settings and situations. As intermediate readers strengthen their reading skills, they become increasingly skilled at independently choosing a "just right" book that grabs their interest.

Middle school and beyond, readers gain experience and progress from "youth" fiction to "adult" fiction. Voracious readers want to discuss, debate and write about their literary explorations.

Ensuring that students are effective readers is an essential component of a well-educated society. In the twenty-first century, public school is a societal construct that must teach humans how to strengthen their connection-making. More than ever before, we need future voters who are able to think critically based on scientific research.

Ascending the Learning to Read Hill to navigate the Reading to Learn Mountains is an ongoing determined quest for Fourth through Twelfth Graders. Thinking critically about what they are reading will continue throughout their lifetime and allows all of us to benefit from cultivating educated citizens and informed voters on into the future.

Back to My Finest Teachers . . .

- *First Grade scientist Malik* exemplified how powerful aligning passions and culturally responsive texts with 'just right books can be as Malik was engaged and persevered more persistently when the books he read were culturally responsive and included characters and plotlines from a variety of cultures. As we learned from partnering with Malik's family, aligning culturally responsive books with his 'just right' level was galvanizing as his cultural identity was important to him.

- *Second Grade artist Sophie* demonstrated the essential understanding that a child's emotional needs are just as important as academics. When Sophie became anxious and angry at the start of the pandemic, she shut down academically. To restart her learning momentum in the midst of a global pandemic, it took a great deal of one-on-one *social-emotional learning* (SEL) support, including coaching Mom and Sophie to establish a range for naming Sophie's emotions (see below), to reteach self-calming and self-regulation before Sophie was able to get back to learning.

- *Third Grade student leader Isabella* reinforced that students need to have their emotional and social needs met to be able to read successfully. When Isabella had increased leadership opportunities at school, she reduced her anxiety by applying her newfound confidence to her reading perseverance. Once her learning momentum with increased practice was underway, she was able to get on track in her learning-to-read journey.

Chapter 4: Momentum Checklist

Reflect: Focusing on Your Finest Teacher (YFT), do a 10-minute write in your Momentum Journal.

- Keeping YFT's strengths and interests in mind, select "just right" books aligned with passions.
- Use successes in whole class lessons, small groups, and IDR to empower continued progress.
- Do you need to continue refining your practice, or identify a new area/skill to focus on (Greene 2020)?
- Review Three Momentum Moves: what should you start doing, stop doing, or continue doing?

Assess:

- Continue listening to YFT regularly so you can responsively adjust "just right" texts as needed.
- Record your ongoing formative assessments as running records so you can track progress.
- Review specific data points and update assessments as needed (for example, DIBLES or F&P).

Plan:

- Review end goal(s) to target both skills and confidence.

- Expect that you will need to explicitly teach children how to work in a group and work independently before you are able to establish effective small group work.
- Expect that even when you have systems well established, they will periodically fall apart during the year, and you will need to get them back on track. Your persistence matters!
- Expect that you will review your Three Momentum Moves for each YFT during the year.
- Plan how you will continuously use YFT's strengths, passions, and superpowers to leverage momentum.

Do: Put your plan into action and monitor how it is going. Refine your systems to meet YFT's emerging needs and your needs as you design efficient, equity-centered systems.

Momentum Checklist

☐ *Reflect*

☐ *Assess*

☐ *Plan*

☐ *Do*

Chapter 5

Teaching the Whole Child: Infusing Social Emotional Learning and Culturally Responsive Teaching into Reading Instruction

"It is vital that when educating our children's brains, we do not neglect to educate their hearts."

—Tenzin Gyatso, 14th Dalai Lama, spiritual leader of Tibetan Buddhism

When I was in Fifth Grade, my family moved, and I started at a new elementary school. There were many times when I felt insecure, lonely, and overwhelmed with trying to "fit in" at my new school. I vividly remember struggling to make new friends, find my way around the school, and catch up in math. Today when I greet new students, I channel my insecure ten-year-old self as I remember how nerve-racking it was for me to go to school every day—and mine was a privileged experience, not impacted by the profound challenges of racism, poverty, intergenerational trauma, or mental health issues. Today, I work hard to remember that I am responsible for teaching the whole child: emotionally, socially, culturally, and academically.

Teaching the Whole Child

No matter whose work you follow—Bloom, Piaget, Adler, Montessori, Hammond, or the Reggio Model — a *whole-child approach explicitly teaches academics alongside emotional regulation, social learning, and cultural understanding and appreciation* via an integrated, research-based approach. The goal of a whole-child approach is to develop a passion for learning through experiential learning, develop authentic relationships with teachers and classmates, and help the child to identify and manage their feelings to develop a greater understanding of the world around them.

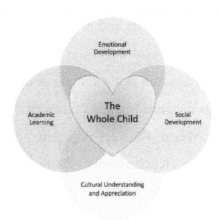

Figure 5.1 by Janine Roy.

Teachers are trained to use research-based instructional practices to develop *academic knowledge and skills*. Chapter 4 focused on how children learn to read. But in addition to instructional moves, educators must simultaneously create belonging through *cultural understanding and appreciation* while supporting students' *emotional and social development*. Explicit instruction in emotional regulation is typically combined into a social-emotional learning (SEL) curriculum, which includes how to self-calm and how regulate emotions throughout the day. Teaching the whole child must also include explicit instruction on identity, understanding and appreciating one's own culture and the cultures of others, developing empathy, and learning about the historical and ongoing impact of racism. Explicit instruction in social skills explores how to make friends, build relationships, and solve problems peacefully.

The concept that it is just as important to explicitly teach children how to self-calm and how make friends as it is to read, write, and do math has been an essential notion for teachers in Canada and many European countries since the 1980s and has expanded in acceptance in the United States with John Mezirow's development of transformative learning theory (Kitchenham 2008). Award-winning international educator and CEP Dr. Gene Carter (2012) stated, "We believe the success of each learner can only be achieved through a whole child approach to learning and teaching."

To give you an idea of what this looks like, let's learn from Sophie and Herman.

Case Study: Sophie

One of My Finest Teachers, First Grade artist Sophie, began at our school in September 2019. An enthusiastic artist, her initial focus was on making friends rather than learning to read. Because she sensed that she was lagging behind her classmates in reading, she, unfortunately, became a skilled reading-avoider and teacher-attention-seeker. Sophie's firm and patient teacher ensured that along with explicit instruction in all academic areas, Sophie and her classmates also received explicit instruction in a social-emotional learning (SEL) curriculum based on Adlerian philosophy incorporated into Jane Nelsen's (2006) model, *positive discipline*. Sophie and her classmates practiced self-calming and mindfulness throughout the day, participated in weekly SEL lessons, had regular class meetings to build vocabulary and understanding of emotions, received explicit instruction to build empathy skills, and practiced solving problems peacefully together using a restorative justice protocol. By March 2020, Sophie knew how to name her feelings using a color-coded Zones of Regulation model (Kuypers 2011), where she named her feelings by aligning them with colors (blue = sad, green = happy). She showed growth in self-regulation and relationship building. She felt belongingness in class and with her classmates.

When Sophie's big feelings about remote learning exploded into tantrums at home, Sophie's mom and I partnered online to practice self-calming strategies, reestablish clear expectations and routines, identify her daughter's initial reading opposition, and strategize the next steps. We worked together to help Sophie name and regulate her feelings by using common language and strategies. For Sophie, her mom and I focused on:

- *Self-awareness—name your feelings.* Since Sophie had learned and was successful in identifying and communicating her emotions using a color-coded Zones of Regulation model (Kuypers 2011) while at school, it became a helpful pandemic intervention strategy to have her "teach" her mom about the process. Partnering with me online empowered Sophie to 'teach' her mom about Zones of Regulation to create a common language and approach. And it motivated her to return to using these familiar SEL strategies.

- *Self-regulation—the importance of teaching how to self-calm and self-manage.* Self-calming is the ability to calm yourself down when you are upset (over-stimulated) or energize yourself when you are tired or distracted (under-stimulated). It requires an awareness of your emotional homeostasis and conscious ability to 'center' oneself. Children and adults alike need to know how to calm their bodies to be in the right 'head space' to learn. Canadian educational researcher Stuart Shanker (2012) wrote about the importance of balancing calm with alertness in his brilliant book, *Calm, Alert, and Learning.* The ability to up-regulate and/or down-regulate our emotions and energy are necessary for all humans, so teaching students how to calm themselves *and* regulate their alertness to maximize learning is key. Kindergartners, high school students to executives all benefit from self-managing their alertness and focusing on new learning at hand to maximize their understanding, retention, application, and evaluation of all the information we encounter daily.
- *Social awareness and relationship skills— getting along with others.* As Sophie and I

worked together to 'teach' her mom to name feelings and follow our school practices, the three of us practiced the concept that in a moment of frustration or anger, use hand signals instead of trying to talk about feelings. As educational researcher Alan November (2012) said, "The person doing the talking is doing the learning," so it was key for Sophie to take the lead to show her mom in order to reinternalize these crucial SEL concepts herself. At school, Sophie learned to communicate her 'big feelings' using the "brain in the palm of your hand" model created by Dr. Daniel Siegel (2011). During 2020 remote learning, her mom and I talked about this model and then brought Sophie into the conversation so Sophie could play the role of teacher. Using Siegal's hand signals and Zones of Regulation concepts consistently made Sophie feel safe as she used the same symbols and language at school and at home. When Sophie was mad, she had a way of effectively communicating her big feelings without words, which reduced and eventually eliminated her pandemic tantrums.

- *Responsible decision-making—reflect, repair, and move forward.* Every big feeling and mistake is a learning opportunity. Instead of seeing a gaffe or a goof as a cataclysmic event, Sophie and her mom learned to see mistakes as learning opportunities and to move forward. Establishing a range to monitor frequency and intensity helped Sophie and her mom becomes better at putting a 'big feelings' moment in perspective. Instead of seeing every daily Home Reading session as a disaster, her mom and I established a 1 to 5 self-rating scale with Sophie, which helped them both put Sophie's explosions in perspective. The scale tracked the intensity and frequency of Sophie's big feelings: 1 was calm, and 5 was the worst disaster ever! Acknowledging and giving language to big feelings helped her mom and Sophie track behavior so Sophie could literally see daily feedback on the intensity and frequency of her tantrums, and this helped Sophie (and her mom) feel more in control. Week by week, as her mom verbally encouraged Sophie's self-regulation, Sophie's Home Reading sessions became more positive. Sophie's outbursts gradually diminished as she began to experience more reading success. Eventually, they didn't need to record the self-rating scale for each session, but the process was a key shifting tool that built momentum for both Sophie and her mom.

A reflection is a powerful tool for teachers and parents. Sophie's mom decided to track her daughter's daily responses to Home Reading time in a *Parent Reflection Journal*. This helped her to identify progress as, over time, she observed that Sophie's procrastination and meltdowns diminished in frequency and intensity. I emphasized that learning to read is a gradual process for every new reader and that Mom could expect that, week by week, things would slowly improve. Just two months later, Sophie proudly read a book to me online that she had read with her teacher and her mom, who reported that the home climate had become much less volatile once Sophie was able to self-regulate her big feelings, which got her back on the learning-to-read track.

Case Study: Herman

In April 2020, the mother of First Grade soccer enthusiast Herman reached out to me at the start of the pandemic to let me know that her bright, enthusiastic son was emphatically balking at home about daily Home Reading. We discussed Herman's struggles with remote learning. Without being able to see his classmates reading the same beginning-to-read books as him, Herman balked at his ascent up the Learning to Read Hill—his fears and frustrations getting in the way of his own learning. By partnering together, Herman's mom and I identified a familiar past experience of Herman's—kicking a soccer ball—and used it as a metaphor that would help him anchor past successful learning experiences with learning to read.

- *Self-awareness and self-regulation.* As Herman's self-regulation was key to building his belongingness, skills, and confidence, in pre-pandemic times, I would have chatted with Herman in the hall to check in on how he was feeling and would have gone to his class to listen to him read. By giving attention and feedback when Herman was successfully self-regulating and practicing his reading with determination, I would have reinforced the behaviors we wanted to see. During a global pandemic, I scheduled regular online meetings with Herman and his mom. In these sessions, Herman discussed his reading fears and worries—a huge "aha" moment for Herman and for his mom and me! I coached him to understand the importance of building his momentum by increasing his perseverance and reading stamina. As he was an enthusiastic soccer player, I aligned his determination to kick a soccer ball accurately with his determination to learn to read.

During scheduled online sessions, Herman's mom and I coached him to articulate his feelings. I gave him a range or scale to describe his feelings[8], set up Independent Reading Time (IDR) in his Visible Daily Schedule, and tracked each time he moved forward to read during IDR with diminished avoidance tactics. By seeing IDR on his Visible Schedule and checking off his reading sessions on a checklist, Herman could see that he was moving forward. We built in some weekly read-aloud sessions together so I could hear him read, and we could all celebrate his successes together.

- *Social awareness and relationship skills.* Because expanding Herman's support network increased his feelings of belonging and trust, we needed to strengthen his connections with us as well as have him see that his mom was

---

[8] To provide young children with language to describe their feelings, I introduce a range of 1 to 5 to help them describe their feelings. "1 is the calmest you have ever felt, and 5 is the angriest you have ever felt, like when you've stubbed your toe." Using hand signals to describe this, such as holding up five fingers on my hand or drawing a range, helps them visualize it. Picturing this range and talking about it gives young children the skills for communicating their feelings to others.

partnering with us. This made him feel like he had a whole team of adults he could trust to help him through his learning-to-read journey. When he struggled in remote learning, I increased my connections with him by meeting with him monthly online for him to read with me and celebrate his progress.

Both before and during the pandemic, Herman received additional reading support from a Reading Specialist three times per week. Herman and his classmates in his Tier II Reading Support group needed extra phonics practice and extra reading practice, and most especially needed to see themselves as readers. To facilitate this in a literal way, his Reading Specialist invited her students to wear a 'reading hat' when reading. Putting on their reading hats not only fostered an identity as a reader but also created belongingness in this small reading group.

Identity and belongingness are powerful, and so are job titles and class jobs. Knowing how this would benefit him, I asked Herman to be one of my Reading Advisors for this book. By "advising" me on my book, he was able to describe his feelings and struggles at the moment and increase his metacognition around learning to read. During our online Reading Advisor sessions, Herman's mom and I partnered to give Herman the time and space to voice his feelings in a productive way by having him use a range or scale to track his feelings. All of these strategies together made a big difference for Herman; his balking diminished as his reading skills and confidence flourished through daily independent reading practice and through his self-reflections as a Reading Advisor.

Getting up the Learning to Read Hill definitely requires a whole child approach. It allows educators and parents to align academic and social-emotional learning (SEL) growth for each child, as the two go hand in hand. Students must be able to self-calm, self-regulate, and get along with others before they can focus on academics. SEL must align with culturally responsive practices to ensure that students feel safe and belong in order to learn (Gray et al., 2018).

Chapter 5: Momentum Checklist

Reflect: Focusing on Your Finest Teacher (YFT), do a 10-minute write in your Momentum Journal.

- Looking at YFT academically, emotionally, and socially, identify areas of strength, areas of growth, and areas you want to work on.
- How can YFT's strengths and interests help with the areas you plan to work on?
- Identify areas of success in whole class lessons, small groups, and IDR. Use successes to empower continued progress.
- Do you need to continue refining your practice, or identify a new area/skill to focus on (Greene 2020)?
- Review Three Momentum Moves: what should you start doing, stop doing, or continue doing?

Assess:

- Continue listening to YFT regularly so you can responsively adjust "just right" texts as needed.
- Record your ongoing formative assessments as running records so you can track progress.
- Review specific data points and update assessments as needed (for example, DIBLES or F&P).

Plan:

- Review end goal(s) to target both skills and confidence.
- Plan how you will support YFT to grow academically, emotionally, and/or socially.
- Expect that you will review your Three Momentum Moves for each YFT during the year.
- Plan how you will continuously use YFT's strengths, passions, and superpowers to leverage momentum.

Do: Put your plan into action and monitor how it is going. Refine your systems to meet YFT's emerging needs and your needs as you design efficient, equity-centered systems.

Momentum Checklist

☐ *Reflect*

☐ *Assess*

☐ *Plan*

☐ *Do*

The How

"A journey of a thousand miles begins with a single step."

—Chinese proverb[9]

---

[9] Chinese proverb from Chapter 64 of the Dao De Jing ascribed to Laozi, although it has been erroneously ascribed to Confucius in the past (Wikipedia.
https://en.wikipedia.org/wiki/A_journey_of_a_thousand_miles_begins_with_a_single_step?scrlybrkr=cb0d5c24).

Chapter 6

Building Momentum through Belonging-Centered Learning

"A deep sense of love and belonging is an irreducible need of all people. We are biologically, cognitively, physically, and spiritually wired to love, to be loved, and to belong. When those needs are not met, we don't function as we were meant to."

—Brené Brown, American research professor and New York Times best-selling author

My first day of Kindergarten: trying bravely not to cry as I said goodbye to my mom while shyly eyeing my new classmates. My first day in Fifth Grade at my new elementary school: a smile on my face but butterflies in my stomach as I tried to remember all the names of my new classmates. My first day as a freshman in high school: striving desperately to find my classes while attempting to look cool. During each of these life moments, I put on a brave face, but I was a wreck inside. My fundamental worry was, "Would I fit in? Would I belong?" Although my feelings reflected their importance, I didn't know then what I know now: belongingness is the essential first step.

Creating Belonging Is the First Step to Building Momentum

Belonging is defined by American educational researcher Carol Goodenow as acceptance, respect, inclusion, and support (Goodenow 1993). Almost 30 years of research (Freeman et al. 2007; Juvonen 2007) support her findings, documenting that...

> ... while teacher and peer support are very impactful on both belonging and achievement, teacher support has the most consistent influence. Note that it is acceptance, not tolerance that is the key.

Belonging is essential for every human's success. If we feel accepted in our environment, we are better able to self-calm and self-regulate. We can build trust, take risks, feel motivated to be kind and helpful, and ultimately learn and strive to do our best (Gray et al. 2018).

To build learning momentum, it is essential that every student and family feels they belong in their learning community. Educational researcher Dr. DeLeon Gray and colleagues created an award-winning framework (Gray et al. 2018) for creating belonging for students since belonging is closely linked to motivation and achievement in school and in life. Gray's research specifically focused on historically marginalized students of color. The framework focuses on creating opportunities for students to feel psychological belonging within their environment (Bowen 2019). Gray's ongoing research indicates that ensuring that students have an authentic voice in their own learning is essential to creating belonging.

Helping Humans Feel Belonging

On the first day of school, creating momentum begins with intentionally infusing every lesson with opportunities for belonging, competence, autonomy, choice, relevance, and cultural relevance.

- *Welcomed and accepted*: Every human needs to feel safe and belong so that they trust those around them enough to take risks and accomplish their goals. Teachers can create classroom communities that feel safe for young humans by creating a welcoming classroom, establishing clear expectations and routines, and explicitly teaching social-emotional learning skills, so students learn equity-centered ways to make friends and solve problems.

- *Competence*: To start a task, stay on task, and finish the task, humans need to feel capable of completing the task successfully in the first place. This is why elementary teachers need to encourage, coach, and cheer on young humans throughout the day. Feeling competent is key to building and maintaining learning momentum.

- *Autonomy*: In its simplest form, autonomy means independence. For elementary children, autonomy is evident when they have age-appropriate independent control over matters they are able to handle, such as putting on their coats, managing their school supplies, or being responsible for a class job. It does not mean having complete freedom to do whatever they want. Autonomy builds life skills and confidence, which fuel learning momentum.

- *Choice*: Giving a choice helps young humans feel that they have some power and control over their environment. At the same time, the choices offered are determined by the teacher. Giving small, limited choices can empower learners to shift their focus and energy to a more positive, productive mindset. The choice is an empowering motivational tool to build learning momentum.

- *Relevance*: Humans are engaged by topics that interest them and/or have meaning to them. Research indicates that if learners can connect new knowledge to prior knowledge, they are able to retain the new learning more effectively (Close, n.d.). By connecting "the known to the new," relevance becomes essential for initiating and sustaining learning momentum.

- *Cultural relevance.* Humans are engaged by topics that are ethnically enriching, interesting, or meaningful to them, as it helps humans to understand and retain information when they can make connections between themselves and the world around them. It doesn't matter whether these connections recognize similarities or differences; making connections builds synapses in the brain, and this is the stepping-stone to the retention and greater understanding. For students of color, cultural relevance is particularly important, as seeing themselves in the books they are reading or discovering a cultural practice that is similar to or different than their own is powerful. Making connections is how humans learn.

Belonging Begins with Relationships

Learning can begin when humans feel safety, belonging, and trust. Ensuring students and families feel welcomed and have connections to classmates and the school leads to trust and achievement. This essential process includes fostering relationships with a student's family. Educational researchers Reich and Mehta reported in Edutopia that "relationships are the key to everything" (Reich and Mehta 2020). It's important to remember that every day, families are bringing their most precious human to school and entrusting us to care for and educate their child. To move forward, educators must explicitly and consistently reach out to families, partner with parents to build relationships, and clearly communicate and create a welcoming, inclusive community.

Using a customer service model, schools can establish explicit welcoming practices and relationship-building initiatives. Canadian educational leader Nella Nelson says, "All learning takes place in relationships" (Nelson 2021).

In 2012–2015, British Columbia's Ministry of Education created the Changing Results for Young Readers framework to gather data collected by 2,000 classroom teachers on 30,000 vulnerable students. The framework identified specific strategies that improved student reading (Delvecchio and Jeroski 2016). I was fortunate to be part of this landmark provincial study.

> The research found that when teachers focused on building belongingness, there was substantial student growth for vulnerable students in self-regulation, confidence (reduced anxiety); personal responsibility and motivation; social awareness and competence; and personal and cultural identity.

Strengthening connections with teachers and peers increased student motivation and increased the student's receptivity to academic interventions, which led to improved student achievement in reading.

Linnenbrink-Garcia's research found that student motivation increased by instructional design that emphasized competence, autonomy, relevance, passion-centered learning, and belonging (Linnenbrink-Garcia et al. 2016). Encouraging feelings of belonging, supporting students' feelings of competence, enhancing student autonomy, identifying tasks that students were passionate about, emphasizing the love of learning, and de-emphasizing social comparisons increased academic and adaptive motivation. Reeve's (2009) research indicated that autonomy-building instructional practices were more motivating than controlling behaviors.

When the pandemic hit, educators faced the monumental task of establishing belonging for students and families in a remote learning environment. This provided an instant opportunity to implement and/or increase culturally responsive and equity-driven practices in classrooms. At the start of the 2020 pandemic, Seattle Public Schools encouraged teachers and school leaders to make pandemic pivots to strengthen student and family connections during remote learning. Staff and I shifted our annual "Welcome Back to School" events to online platforms to connect with families. As consistent communication became more important to families than ever before, staff and I maintained our weekly updates to families with determination and passion. Online family surveys identified remote learning needs and want. Fall and winter webinars offered parents the opportunity to collaborate and learn together with other families. Family questionnaires gathered ongoing feedback. November Parent–Teacher Conferences partnered with families to continuously refine our practices, as parents became monumentally valued experts on their child's learning team. Throughout the school year, I met with families in Town Hall formats, webinars, and online meetings to stay connected. When learning challenges were encountered, it was the teacher-student relationship and home–school partnership that got learning back on track and continued to build momentum.

"Moving at the Speed of Trust"

The goal of building belonging for students and families is to establish trust. As discussed in Chapter 3, trust is essential as teachers, schools, and districts can only "move at the speed of trust" (Covey 2005).

> Educators, schools, and school districts must take note that the essential component of belongingness for students and families is to strengthen trust between home and school.

Seattle Public Schools illuminated the power of building belongingness with students and families through the district's equity-driven initiatives over the past decade. In 2018, Chief Academic Officer Dr. Keisha Scarlett and Chief Officer of African American Male Achievement Dr. Mia Williams led innovative district-wide initiatives that specifically focused on implementing assets-based programs and policies to increase the belongingness and achievement of African American students. The pandemic accelerated this crucial equity-driven work. In 2020, they increased district-wide initiatives to reimagine schools (Reich and Mehta 2020) and increased opportunity structures (Gray et al.

2018). Guided by Covey's (2005) "speed of trust" mantra, Scarlett (2020) realized that not only couldn't the district pander to white supremacy, district staff also had to build belongingness and trust with students and families of color.

Scarlett's own research found that "many U.S. schools rest on a Eurocentric platform that promotes policies, practices, and curricula that devalue and marginalize Black brilliance, self-expression, history, innovation, and societal contributions." Citing the 2014 research of Ladson-Billings (2014), Scarlett inspired educators to focus on academic success, cultural competence, and sociopolitical consciousness to increase belongingness, motivation, and academic achievement. She reported that this movement involved "tapping into the strength of community" to establish and fortify family partnerships to drive racial justice.

Gray's Structures for Building Belonging in Communities

Over the past several decades, studies documented that students who feel that they belong at their school generally do well academically and emotionally (Freeman et al., 2007). Gray et al.'s 2018 study documented that student belongingness leads to motivation, and motivation is key to learning. When I met with Dr. Gray, he explained that he deeply believed that being culturally connected to one's community was important, especially during childhood—and his research supported this concept.

Gray's research focused on belongingness, autonomy, choice, relevance, and competence, and specifically focused on:

- *Interpersonal belonging opportunities*: activities and initiatives that help each student feel that they belong among their peers and are welcomed and accepted by staff. Interpersonal belonging is the first step to building learning momentum, and it is the stepping-stone to instructional belonging and institutional belonging.

- *Instructional belonging opportunities*: strategies and systems that help each student to feel belonging, safety, and trust in class. Elementary educators foster instructional belonging when they teach young humans how to independently manage their school supplies, transition in an orderly manner from one space to another, be responsible for classroom jobs, put away the math game, and get out their pencils. Middle and high school educators teach students how to independently manage their binders, textbooks, and homework assignments.

- *Institutional belonging opportunities*: school and school district systems and policies that help students and their families feel welcomed and safe in their school community. From a user-friendly enrollment platform to schoolwide events to providing translators with ease, school districts need to establish equity-centered practices, review current practices with an equity-driven lens, and dismantle and eliminate racist practices. This is essential, decades-long work.

Gray's research reinforced what I had observed throughout my career: when students feel safe and trusting in class, feel that they belong among their peers in class and on the playground, and feel that they and their families are welcomed in their school community, then the student is set

How to Build Belonging

Keeping the end in mind throughout the year, teachers plan each lesson and also craft opportunities to build and strengthen belonging every day:

- *Welcomed and accepted*: When students arrive in the morning, greet each student at the door and make an interpersonal connection (for example, "How did your soccer game go last night?" "I notice you are wearing your favorite shirt today!"). Establish class expectations where mistakes are welcomed, so cheering on rather than criticizing classmates is the norm. Establish a system of making small moments of connection throughout the day, especially for students furthest from educational justice.[10] Set up informal opportunities for students to partner with a classmate, do a job together, or work in a small group with supportive peers.

- *Competence*: Humans often need to feel capable in order to undertake a task. To foster a growth

---

[10] One strategy is the '2 × 10 Strategy': for two minutes each day, intentionally have an informal chat with a specific student for 10 days. Chat about whatever the student wants to discuss, as this is their time with you. This is an opportunity to build interpersonal belonging and connect with another fabulous student. My recommendation: don't stop after 10 days, as this can become a moment of professional joy to connect with a young human.

mindset and an "I can do it attitude," teachers need to identify students' strengths and help them use these "superpowers" to foster their feelings of competence. This generates both interpersonal and instructional belonging. If a student feels overwhelmed by a task and is afraid to start, it is the job of the teacher to scaffold the task so the student can feel successful. If the student gets halfway through an assignment and stalls due to confusion or lack of impetus, the teacher needs to help them get back on track by breaking down the task further to help the child get the task done. When students finish a task, it is important for the teacher to reinforce the student's capability to accomplish a goal to reinforce their confidence and encourage future task completion.

- *Autonomy*: Foster independence by teaching students how to manage their school supplies or help with classroom jobs. Scheduling regular class meetings give space for students to share ideas and seek solutions together. Middle and high school educators teach students how to independently manage their binders, textbooks, and homework assignments. Autonomy builds

145

life skills and confidence, which fuel learning momentum.

- *Choice*: Teacher-determined choices can foster both interpersonal and instructional belonging. Establish schoolwide initiatives such as leadership opportunities, clubs, and teams to foster equity-centered institutional belonging within the school community. For example, when the Kindergartner is having a meltdown and needs to take a break, offering the small option of either taking a break at their seat or in the Class Calm Spot, and limiting the choices to two, can provide the necessary locus of control to help them pivot to calm down, cool off, and reset their brain and their body.

- *Relevance*: Making connections, whether it is with a new friend or with something they are reading, generates feelings of interpersonal and instructional belonging. Starting each lesson linking "the new to the known" establishes and strengthens synaptic connections, just as students noticing the similarities and differences between themselves and a friend establishes social connections and strengthens belonging. Helping students make culturally relevant connections impacts all learners, especially learners of color. While primary students may compare the characters of Frog and Toad, or intermediate, middle, and high schoolers may contrast the theme of two novels, the act of making connections deepens their understanding of the importance of what they are learning.

Building and strengthening belonging are essential for every human every day.

Five Ideas for Building Interpersonal Belonging

1. *Develop a relationship with every student.*
   - *Before-the-school-year-commences*: Before the school year begins, finding out as much as possible about every student is key. Talking with colleagues, looking at school records, reviewing Individual Education Plans, and attending a school "meet and greet" with families are all essential to-dos for getting ready to welcome every student with open arms.

   - *On the first day of school*: From the very first minute, let every student know you can't wait to get to know them and are excited to have them in your class. The first day is focused on getting to know each human. First-day icebreaker activities can simultaneously work on routines and allow you to observe peer interactions. On the first day, strive to learn one thing about every student. In the first week, call each student's family to introduce yourself and tell them how much you are looking forward to getting to know their child and looking forward to the year ahead. While these calls take time, it is essential to begin the year with a positive interaction. [11]After school, use your class list to record which students you can picture when you see their names and one fact about each student, and then make sure to focus on the remaining students the following day so that your mission of building relationships is thoughtful and intentional.

- *By the end of the first week*: The teacher has guided students to mutually establish clear expectations/agreements.[12] These remain posted

---

[11] Calling families to introduce yourself and tell them how much you are looking forward to getting to know their child and looking forward to the year ahead takes time, and it is absolutely time well spent. It means the first home–school contact is positive, and teachers can partner with families from the start.

[12] Involving students in setting class agreements or expectations are nuanced, as teachers have a clear plan of their expectations, and it

throughout the year as they become the guide and guardrails. If the teacher has called every parent, knows every student's name, and knows one thing about every student, then children are set up for success. If they feel welcomed, accepted, and safe, they will be ready to learn.

- *Center instruction on equity-centered, culturally responsive practices*: Every student and their family need educators to be both culturally responsive practitioners and social justice champions. Implementing research-based inclusive practices throughout the year benefits all students. To ensure that learning is equity-centered and culturally responsive for every student, use multicultural books and resources that celebrate a variety of cultures, recognize and celebrate a variety of cultural celebrations throughout the year, and teach worldview history rather than Eurocentric history by using resources such as The 1619 Project, Facing History and Ourselves, and Abolitionist Teaching Network. Explicitly teaching students about race, racism, and anti-racist practices creates

---

builds community and fosters student autonomy if their voices are included.

149

awareness of past unjust practices and help global citizens to be culturally responsive, equity-driven, and effective social justice champions. For specific ideas, look to educational experts Na'ilah Suad Nasir et al. (2018), Zaretta Hammond (2015), and Dr. Gholdy Muhammad (2020).

- *Identify student strengths, interests, and needs*: As teachers get to know students and develop a relationship with their families at the start of the year, the goal is to partner with families to identify student strengths, interests, and needs. Conduct self-assessments, survey families, talk with colleagues—continuously get to know these humans! Their strengths are their superpowers that you will acknowledge, build upon, and celebrate throughout the year.

- *Partner with families throughout the year*: Continue surveying students and families throughout the year to seek input and build safety and trust, as students need to feel safe before they can take risks to learn. Teachers asking for feedback establishes a safe classroom climate and leads to teachers being able to provide feedback to students in a safe, trusting environment. Student surveys, feedback forms, exit tickets, reflection journals, Padlet boards— continuous feedback is the ticket to helping Your Finest Teacher get up the Learning to Read Hill.

2. *What you feed will grow.* As we establish a relationship with each student, it is the teacher's job and school leader's job to nurture this relationship to build belongingness and trust. Frequent personal connections throughout the day with students help them feel safe and loved. Checking in to have a quick chat is the first step. A teacher's superpower is "noticing" when we see expected/desired behaviors, then focusing our "attention laser beam" to reinforce these desired positive behaviors. At the same time, ignoring unwanted behaviors is essential, too, as we want to reinforce expected behaviors and not give our attention to unwanted behaviors. While teachers need to redirect or address unsafe behaviors, adults need to be aware of what we are reinforcing, as what we "feed" will "grow," for example, "I noticed you were working hard to read that page." "I saw you go back and reread that word when it didn't make sense. That's what readers do!" "I watched you

persevere even when this word was tricky. That's what readers do!"

3. *If my family trusts you, I will trust you.* Having an interpersonal connection with each family is a top goal for teachers and school leaders. This is a symbiotic relationship; as the child gets to know the teacher, and the teacher gets to know the child and their family, with authentic efforts on the part of educators, families will hopefully move toward building trust with the teacher and the school. If the family feels trust, then they will be more likely to partner with the school, and this, in turn, increases feelings of connection and support at school. Understandably, this may take longer for families experiencing long-standing inequities in school systems. Schools need to be prepared so that home–school relationships must be initiated and nurtured by teachers and principals. Each family has given teachers and principals the gift of sharing their most important human in the world with us each day. Educators have the privilege of spending time with their children. Teachers have the privilege of watching their children discover, learn, and grow. Principals and teachers have the privilege of putting a band-aid on their child's knee, listening to their

child's stories, hearing their child's worries, loving their child unconditionally, and watching their child flourish. It is an honor and a privilege to have each child at school every day. Educators need to embrace that it is a privilege and responsibility to build belongingness and trust with children and families.

4. *Reflect on relationships daily.* How are we building trust with each student? How are we strengthening our relationships with families? How are we collaborating and partnering with colleagues? Educators must constantly think about how we can build and sustain our relationships with our students and their families, and our colleagues throughout the year.

5. *Collaboration is key.* Working together has a powerful impact on adult momentum and, ultimately, on student achievement. The process of partnering with families to learn each child's strengths, interests, and needs is essential—since parents know their child best—as is teachers and school leaders collaboratively creating and refining equity-centered systems, strategies, and practices that work for individual students and their families. As author George Couros (2015) says about collaboration,

"The smartest person in the room is the room." Collaboration empowers the development of creative solutions that work.

A child who feels interpersonal connections and acceptance in the classroom feels belongingness in the school. When the child feels safe and belonging, he/she/they will take risks. And you need to take risks to learn to read. When a child feels they belong, this strengthens a family's feelings of belonging in the school community and, hopefully, builds trust. Belongingness and trust of students and families are essential starting points, as it is from here that momentum and academic success build.

Three Ideas for Building Instructional Belonging

Instructional belongingness is when a child feels safe and trusted enough to take educational risks and persevere. To achieve this, we need to implement instructional practices that provide support for both skill development and confidence building. Structures provide daily classroom support for skill development and confidence building. Here are three examples of how it works from a student's point of view:

1. *If I feel welcomed and belonging in my classroom, I will trust my teacher*. Welcoming environments

create a climate of acceptance and community. Building relationships between teacher and student, and student with classmates, create feelings of safety and trust. Together, this fosters a safe place to learn. Since centuries-long racism and bigotry within U.S. educational systems is a great barrier to trust, educators must have patience and perseverance with the process, understanding that history may be a deterrent. And that the only way is to continuously build and sustain these relationships.

2. *If I trust my teacher, I will begin my learning momentum by being helpful, taking learning risks, and persevering.* Learning to read involves confidence, taking risks, making mistakes, and persevering even when it is difficult. Creating opportunities for building confidence, such as creating a rotating list of class jobs, so every student has daily responsibilities, offering a familiar task where they feel successful, or trying something slightly different but not too tricky, can build feelings of success, which is a good step toward building and sustaining momentum.

3. *If I feel successful, I will accelerate my momentum by working harder, being more flexible, and being*

more accepting of others. As Olympian and American soccer superstar Mia Hamm says, "Success breeds success." We all want to do things we are good at and enjoy. The more teachers and school leaders help a student to feel successful, then the more the student's momentum will build. This is why daily "noticing" comments are so powerful! Help all of your students identify as readers by frequently stating, "Xen, I see you are working hard at reading every day! You are a determined reader!" "Ziv, I noticed you went back to make sure it made sense! That's what critical thinkers do!" "Lee, I see you persevering! You are a voracious reader!"

Three Ideas for Building Institutional Belonging

Institutional belonging ensures that every student feels like an accepted, valued member of the learning community; this will empower learners to build and accelerate their learning momentum toward becoming a reader and empowered global citizens. Effective, research-based schoolwide systems include:

1. *Research-based, balanced literacy programs*. These provide every student with explicit instruction in comprehension, phonics, and vocabulary development. A solid program consistently

156

emphasizes the importance of daily reading practice. Explicitly build independent reading practice into daily schedules.

2. *Celebrating reading stamina in class and schoolwide.* Develop and celebrate perseverance as a life skill. Reading stamina is the amount of time a young student can stay on task while reading independently. Tracking this as a class by graphing each day's Independent Reading Time (IDR) allows the teacher to celebrate the collective perseverance and to read stamina students are building. (Graphing independent time is a great primary math activity too!) Tracking IDR is never used to single a student out nor focus on the differing levels of "just right" books being read in the class. Instead, it helps students feel part of something powerful and celebrates their incremental successes. The goal of tracking IDR is to recognize that reading practice is essential, highlight the importance of perseverance, and increase the collective self-awareness of their perseverance. Plan celebratory events like class pajama parties, dance party Friday, or schoolwide events like "double recess"[13] to recognize the growth

---

[13] Double recess is just what it sounds like—it is shifting the schoolwide schedule on one specific day, so students have twice as much time playing outside. Students are highly motivated to work

in the collective's Independent Reading Time minutes. Stamina improves reading!

3. *Communicate that reading is a top school priority during events, assemblies, and school newsletters.* Champion daily independent reading practice at both home and school. Setting up a schoolwide Home–School Reading program helps to ensure that every reader has equitable practice systems to support them, which include "just-right" texts, a Home–School folder for carrying these books between home and school, communication mechanism so the parent can communicate with the teacher, parent education, so families know how to read at home with their child to reinforce targeted skills, and school-based systems to provide extra practice if a family is unable to practice at home. Invite families to share photos of their child reading to use in newsletters, as well as on social media. Broadcast collective reading growth in school assemblies. Snap photos during Buddy Reading, Library classes, and in classrooms to reinforce the school's collective commitment to improving reading. Schoolwide events are powerful

---

toward this phenomenally powerful goal. It takes a bit of figuring as a principal, but it is well worth it—a few minutes extra of fresh air and exercise is always a joyful achievement, and it reinforces the community's value of perseverance and collaboration.

ways to celebrate our reading identity and our collective achievement; focusing on minutes read puts all students on an equitable playing field so that the focus is on hard work, not reading level.

Belonging is a powerful force for all humans. We are driven to seek acceptance and love, and if we find it, we are able to progress up Maslow's hierarchy to learn. Helping each child to feel that they belong is an essential first step to building, sustaining, and accelerating their learning momentum.

Learning from My Finest Teachers . . .

- *Kindergarten scientist Malik* and his family taught us that a child who feels safe and connected at school is far more likely to feel motivated about learning, take risks, persevere, and make academic progress. Based on his positive relationship with his teacher in both Kindergarten and First Grade, Malik clearly felt connected and safe. He felt supported by the partnership between his family and his school. If there was a tricky book to read at home at night, Mom would reinforce his perseverance. As classroom jobs were assigned to every member of his class, Malik had daily opportunities to be helpful and build his confidence through leadership and service. Malik exemplified the concept that being a leader and being of service in one's community is, according to Gray (2021), "the secret sauce" of student success. By the end of First Grade, Malik was exceeding expectations in reading.

- *First Grade math enthusiast Luis* and his family taught me that passions are powerful vehicles for building belongingness and motivation. His love of science and feelings of expertise in math gave us vehicles for linking his "just right" books with areas he was passionate about. His mom partnered with us to encourage Luis to read at home using his high-interest, low vocabulary science-based nonfiction books. Over time, he became an avid reader. By the end of First Grade, Luis was meeting expectations in reading.

- The key to reducing *Second Grade artist Sophie*'s anxiety and reading avoidance was to strengthen our relationship with Sophie and her mom. As Sophie's behavior aligned with the educational worries she overheard at home, strengthening home–school relationships was essential. Once she felt safe at school because she knew Mom trusted her teacher, Sophie was able to follow the firm and kind expectations set for her in class and take risks to read increasingly harder books, and Mom was able to support her daughter's progress through encouragement at home. And then, the pandemic hit, and we had to rebuild relationships and trust all over again in a remote environment. Reestablishing relation-ships online enabled Sophie to resume independent reading practice each day. By mid–Second Grade, Sophie was meeting expectations in reading.

- Leadership opportunities were key to *Third Grade student leader Isabella*'s belonging and confidence. Helping younger children on the playground at lunch as a Student Playground Coach helped Isabella feel confident and focused during daily IDR. Her parents cheered on Isabella's reading success at home. Increased confidence led to increased practice, which resulted in increased reading achievement. Through collaborative home–school partnership, increasing belongingness and trust, and establishing a Personalized Empowerment

Project, Isabella was meeting expectations in reading by the end of Third Grade.

Chapter 6: Momentum Checklist

Reflect: In your Momentum Journal, think about the opportunities you offer and strategies you use that build belonging. Record the actions you are taking to build interpersonal belongingness and instructional belongingness with Your Finest Teacher. As a school leader, identify how you are building institutional belongingness in your community. As a human, reflect on how you are moving at the speed of trust with students, families, and colleagues.

Assess:

- To build belonging, ask questions, conduct student surveys, and seek student input on Padlet.
- Seek parental input through questionnaires to identify student strengths and interests.
- Ask for student feedback to build trust and model the importance of their input.

- Review specific data points and update assessments as needed (for example, DIBLES[14] or F&P[15]).

Plan:

- Choose one or more ideas for building interpersonal belonging.
- When YFT is demonstrating they feel interpersonal belonging, choose one or more ideas for building instructional belonging.
- When YFT demonstrates instructional belonging, choose one or more ideas for building institutional belonging.
- Plan how you will support YFT to grow academically, emotionally, and/or socially.
- Expect that you will review your Three Momentum Moves for each YFT during the year.
- Plan how you will continuously use YFT's strengths, passions, and superpowers to leverage momentum.

---

[14] DIBLES, or Dynamic Indicator of Basic Literacy Skills, is University of Oregon's tool to assess the acquisition of literacy skills. These assessments are intended to be one-minute fluency measures designed to identify struggles early, allowing teachers to responsively provide differentiated instruction to meet individual beginning readers' needs. https://dibels.uoregon.edu/.
[15] Fountas and Pinnell (F&P) provide a fluency and reading comprehension tool for benchmarking reading levels in order to ensure that students are provided with text that is "just right" for them so they can read with accuracy. https://www.heinemann.com/collection/fp.

Do: Put your plan into action and monitor how it is going. Refine your systems to meet YFT's emerging needs and your needs as you design efficient, equity-centered systems.

Momentum Checklist

☐ *Reflect*

☐ *Assess*

☐ *Plan*

☐ *Do*

Chapter 7

Accelerating Momentum

"If you can't fly, then run.
If you can't run, then walk.
If you can't walk, then crawl.
But whatever you do,
you have to keep moving forward."
—Dr. Martin Luther King

One April day, when Isabella was in Second Grade, she arrived in the school office bringing a perceived playground problem to my attention, which I knew was her secret strategy to avoid IDR right after lunch. At that very moment, I was needed elsewhere, so I asked Isabella to sit with a group of Kindergarteners having lunch while I helped the others. By the time I returned, Isabella had the Kindergartners calmly eating their lunch as she regaled them with her stories and jokes. Suddenly, I discovered a new Student Playground Coach for the next year! In the fall, Third Grader Isabella and a friend chose to eat lunch early so they could be Playground Coaches during the younger students' lunch block. They missed zero instructional time, they became adored Student Playground Coaches, and they arrived back in class after lunch feeling great and ready to read during right-after-lunch IDR. Isabella's reading procrastination evaporated as her leadership, reading skills, and confidence increased. Keeping your eyes open for the right opportunity is essential—and, oh, so rewarding!

Accelerating Learning Momentum

Isabella highlighted to me that momentum-building opportunities are everywhere at school. As author Farshad Asl (2016) said, "It takes a massive action to build on the momentum, and it takes self-discipline to sustain the momentum." But you have to keep your eyes open and seize the opportunity, as they don't normally hit you over the head as Isabella's did. Carpe diem—seize the day!

This chapter explores Three Momentum Moves to cumulatively accelerate individual learning momentum for students furthest from educational justice and simultaneously dismantle systemic racist practices to nurture and empower all students. By working differently, educators can strengthen belongingness, get students on track faster, reduce classroom conflicts, put teaching energy into positive practices, and empower student learning and our professional joy. Ultimately, putting a variety of equity-driven strategies in place for Your Finest Teachers will accelerate their learning momentum.

Implementing Three Momentum Moves: A Comprehensive Intervention Plan

Three Momentum Moves is a comprehensive, whole-child intervention plan implemented in collaboration with colleagues and families:

1. *Center learning on belongingness, trust, and passion.* Children need to feel connected to teachers, peers, and their learning community. Children feel safe when their teacher partners with their family, as it feels supportive when they have a unified Home–School Team supporting them. Every student needs to feel belonging at school and feel loved and appreciated for their unique contributions to the learning community. Every student should have opportunities for autonomy, choice, and learning about topics that are relevant to them. To feel confident, every child needs to feel competent, so teachers may need to differentiate and scaffold activities to set children up for success. Confident learners are empowered to take learning risks and persevere, and this ultimately empowers them to

169

make an authentic difference for others and in the world around them.

2. *Partner with colleagues and parents.* Teachers, school leaders, and families working together can create authentic home-school partnerships to support every learner. Partnering with every family is important, but partnering with families whose children need more practice is essential.

3. *Increase practice to build momentum and improve reading.* As Hammond (2015) says, "practice makes permanent." Increasing reading practice by combining a balanced literacy program with daily independent reading practice augmented by additional reading practice at home can ensure that home–school independent reading practice strategies are aligned and systematic.

Diving in Deeper . . .

We looked closely at what was working for Malik so we could learn from it and apply these successful concepts to help other students. As My Finest Teachers, First Grader Luis, First Grader Sophie, and Third Grader Isabella exemplified the power of Three Momentum Moves. Let's dive deeper into each of the Three Momentum Moves to see how these actions helped each student become a reader and a leader at school.

First Momentum Move: Center Learning on Belonging and Trust

Momentum is accelerated by increasing efforts to simultaneously strengthen relationships with students and families and incorporating students' passions and interests into learning.

Here are some tried and true strategies for centering learning on belongingness, trust, and passion:

Home–School Partnership Initiatives: A key first step in developing and strengthening home-school partnerships is through annual school events, as they offer during and after-hours opportunities for families to see their child's learning in action. "Welcome Back to School" events, "Meet the Teacher Night," Parent–Teacher Conferences, Science Night, and Spring Fair are all examples of events that schools have those welcome families to partner and celebrate student learning.

Help with Friendships: Some kids may make friends easily, and some may need some support from staff. Increase belongingness by explicitly teaching friendship-making

171

skills. Integrate the SEL curriculum with Language Arts curriculum to explicitly teach social skills, friendship skills, and effective social problem-solving in class. Beyond using books to develop self-awareness, social awareness, and relationship skills, partner a friend-seeking student with a helpful classmate, ask them to do an errand with a peer, or connect one of Your Finest Teachers with a classmate who has a similar interest. Also, don't underestimate the power of a few kind words from you, as this may help a student bridge the gap between being the kid on the sidelines to the classmate in the center of recess adventures.

Passion Projects: Once you identify a student's strengths and interests, nurture their interests to build student learning momentum. Help them find books on their hobby of the moment; this may last an afternoon or a lifetime. Talk with them about their passion, so they feel like an expert. Incorporate their interests into book selections, math problems, science experiments, nature walks—the sky is the limit!

Scribing Empowers Learners: Scribing, the act of an adult writing down the dictated words of a student is a phenomenally liberating tool as it lets students share their thoughts without the cognitive load of writing. It is 100% liberating for students, especially those who struggle with writing. Student A may have a fantastic topic sentence, but they may need help with actually writing it down. Student B may not know how to get started, but with the teacher picking up the pencil and being willing to write down the first few sentences, this gets the writing process underway. Even better, record their dictation at their "just right" reading level, and voilà—they have a "just right" book that they authored!

Second Momentum Move: Partner with Colleagues and Families

Partnerships matter. The two types of partnerships that are essential are partnering with colleagues and partnering with families. Teachers working together with colleagues and with families create a powerful synergy. Ideas tend to be better when we shape them together. Remember Couros's (2015) wisdom that "the smartest person in the room is the room!" Look to Chapter 8 and Chapter 9 for a close examination of collaborative strategies. By working together, our ideas and our practices are better, deeper, and richer.

Following are some effective partnering strategies:

Partner with Colleagues: It is personally and professionally satisfying to work with others to accomplish a common goal. K through 12 teachers can join school-based and/or district-based collaboration structures to organize

173

events, become part of committees, and join Professional Learning Networks (PLNs). It is essential for groups to be ever-evolving and make explicit efforts to welcome all voices.

Partner with Families: Connect with families to identify student strengths, interests, and needs:

- *September family questionnaires.* Sent out as hard copies or via e-mail, this help to identify student strengths, needs, and interests. Short-answer queries such as "Identify your child's strengths" and "Share some of your child's interests" gather essential data for the year from the humans who are experts about their child. Make it easy and accessible but leave plenty of space for comments as you want as much information as you can get!

- *Pick up the phone!* Based on first-day observations, make proactive, positive phone calls to every student's family to introduce yourself. I recommend calling attention-seeking students first, keeping in mind that even if something unexpected happens at school, this call should still stay positive. Since it is important to establish this connection of positivity before the first "learning opportunity" arises, make these calls in the first few days of school, half of the class on the first day and the rest on the following day. They need only be two-to-three-minute calls to establish a connection. A phone call is more personal, but if you can't reach the parent, then go ahead and e-mail or text. If you can't reach the family, go to your administrator/counselor/vice principal/school secretary to make sure you have every emergency number—and try them too. Also, you don't want to be missing contact info in an emergency, and you need to know if a student's home situation has changed over the summer. With multilingual families, ensure translation support is available.

- *Regular communications.* Ensure families are well informed about their child's progress through continued and regular schoolwide communications. Weekly class newsletters provide current information on initiatives and upcoming activities and celebrate learning happening around the school. This is key to sustaining a healthy home-school partnership. For individual students on a Home–School

Reading Plan, establish a Home–School Book Log to share information about books read, and give space for families to share feedback on how nightly reading is going.

- *Celebrate successes!* Acknowledging when success happens, celebrating safe choices made, and cheering on students when they resolve conflicts peacefully are the day-to-day strategies for helping build a child's learning momentum. Sending a Friday celebratory e-mail for an individual student, making a quick call home to celebrate the learning opportunity of the day, or checking in with a parent at morning drop-off are all ways to celebrate the small and big successes of each day to reinforce behaviors we want to foster.

Third Momentum Move: Increase Practice to Build Momentum and Improve Reading

As educational researcher Richard Allington (2006) said, "75% of kids learn to read in spite of us; 25% of kids learn to read because of us." The increasing practice has a significant impact on the "because of us" kids. Adapted from Allington's research, a 3-T IDR model is recommended:

Team with families to build the student's and family's relationship with the school.

1. *Time*: Partner with your wise parental advisors and colleagues to increase reading practice time. Work together to develop a Home–School Plan. Identify what works best for the family, which could include extra independent reading practice at school or at home, or both. If extra practice is solely happening at school, make sure the family knows the weekly progress status so they can cheer on their child.

2. *Text*: Based on ongoing running records, provide the decodable "just right" text the student is ready for. A few minutes per day gradually extended to 30 minutes of IDR builds brain cells, fuels confidence with endorphins, and motivates readers to get up the Learning to Read Hill.

Understanding the Three Momentum Moves is the first step. Next, we need . . .

Strategies to Accelerate Momentum

Independent Daily Reading Time (IDR): Daily time for independent reading is an integral component of a research-based reading instructional program. Teachers need to anchor IDR in the daily schedule and explicitly work with the class to build reading stamina. This takes time, patience, practice, and a keen eye to know when to end IDR, as a wise teacher ends IDR before the student with the least stamina derails the opportunity. Figuring out ways for each student to feel success is the focus, including finding culturally responsive books students can read at their level, setting firm boundaries and clear expectations, outlining small, easy-to-achieve goals with gradually increased expectations, and cheering them on every step of the way.

Create a Visible Schedule: It builds safety and trust when everyone has a "mental map" of the day and can follow predictable routines. Post a schedule that is visible to the whole class that lists Independent Daily Reading Time to reinforce the importance of daily practice routines. Some students may benefit from having the visible schedule taped to their desks.

Use Visual Cues and Reinforcements: Reinforce the behavior you want to continue; how you pay attention matters! Nonverbal cues reinforce expected behaviors and can avoid verbal conflicts. When a child is following a schedule (even briefly!), walk by and record a checkmark on the schedule or give them a private signal to visually reinforce the child's on-task behavior without derailing it. Snap a photo of the check mark to share it with family; this gives another positive reinforcement for the student at home. If a student is off task, a teacher can walk by and tap the schedule to cue returning to schedule; redirection through a visual cue such as this can be more effective for some students (and less authoritarian) than verbal directives. (It can build connection and autonomy for some young humans if they have a nonverbal "secret signal" with the teacher to get started, as some young humans resist, avoid, or become oppositional if they are told point blank to get started.)

Implement a Daily Checklist: Creating a "daily checklist" and taping it at the student's desk can build autonomy and connection with the teacher as the student receives attention and feedback each time an item is marked off. Clearly, listing what needs to be done is an effective organizational skill, and the opportunity to mark items off on a checklist feels satisfying. Communicating checklist completion to the family can also reinforce and celebrate desired behaviors.

Establish Home–School Reading Plan: After using a reading assessment tool to determine independent reading levels (a "just right" book that can be read with 95% accuracy) and instructional reading levels (a book that can be read with 90% accuracy), if it is evident that a student would benefit from extra reading practice, meet with the family to partner on how to increase reading practice. For some families, a Home–School Reading Plan may work with family schedules; for others, it may not, so the teacher may need to set up extra practice at school. Figure out the details together and agree to regularly check in to see how things are going.

- *Provide decodable "just right" texts*: These are books to read at home and school based on each student's independent reading level.

- *"Short and sweet" practice*: Daily reading practice at home should be "short and sweet" for the developing reader: five to 10 minutes spent reading books at their independent reading level builds skills, confidence, and reading stamina. This routine practice needs to provide positive reinforcement for the student without feeling onerous for either the child or the parent. (See Chapter 10 for more information about the power of practice.)

- *Monitor progress through feedback*: Communications are essential in the home–school partnerships. The teacher and family work

180

out an efficient book exchange system and set up a super-simple system for the parent to share how things are going. This system works!

- *Voice and choice*: A student has "dessert books" to read daily after "just right" books. This becomes a key "when/then" protocol, as students can be highly motivated to read "just right" books so they can peruse "dessert" books.

Use Encouragement versus Praise: For students like Sophie, specific verbal encouragement ("I noticed you worked hard on writing your paragraph.") was more effective than general judgmental praise ("Good job!"). Nonverbal cues can work, too, such as ignoring unwanted behavior for 30 seconds and then redirecting it if necessary. Giving specific encouragement when a task is completed is important!

Provide Extra Support: Additional support via explicit instruction, small reading group support, extra practice, and specific encouragement will improve a child's reading skills. If there isn't allocated staff to provide this support, invite and train parent reading volunteers and community group volunteers to give extra one-on-one support in reading to the learners who need it.

Use a "When/Then Plan": This method sets clear expectations and routines to ensure the student completes the non-preferred task before completing the preferred task. The "then" option is determined by the adult to ensure it is developmentally appropriate and specific. For example, when a student finishes IDR, they have the autonomy and choice to either read "dessert books" and/or help a peer pick a dessert book; this choice is manageable for the child and teacher. It builds reading skills and confidence when they have adult-determined choices aligned with strengths and interests.

Create a Personalized Passion Project and/or Leadership Opportunity: Creating a passion project tailored to a student's interest can propel motivation to take learning risks, persevere, and confidently learn to read. By recognizing that Isabella was a natural leader, we chose Student Playground Coach to be her passion project. As First Grade math enthusiast Luis often finished his math task quickly, inviting him to be a Math–Science Coach in class to encourage his classmates became his passion project. Second Grade artist Sophie's opportunity to join an Art Club at lunch filled her heart with joy and motivated her to read with determination. See Chapter 11 for details on passion projects.

Celebrate! Tracking IDR time is an authentic math activity and can build community. A teacher can schedule a class celebration each time the class reaches a specific pre-agreed, teacher-determined milestone. An example at my school: A Class Pajama Party involved coming to school in pajamas/cozy clothes and having a longer IDR that day. Seriously, this is a powerful motivational strategy for primary readers!

If the Momentum Moves and strategies above seem like a lot of work, think of these steps as different work rather than more work. By working differently, we can share the load, get students on track faster, reduce our emotional energy of reminding/nagging, reduce classroom conflicts, and empower students and teachers who are empowered by student success.

As you implement these strategies, self-coaching is important, as Atomic Habits author James Clear (2018) notes that it takes six to eight weeks to establish a new habit. Patience and persistence are essential! When implementing strategies to strengthen interpersonal and instructional belongingness for YFT:

- *Look for any approximation of desired behavior*: If YFT is able to read independently for two minutes, then set IDR for them for two minutes and gradually extend IDR for them to three minutes, and then celebrate each minute added as a monumental achievement. Make each small step forward a "big deal" as YFT moves up the Learning to Read Hill!

- *Give it time*: Be persistent; try a strategy for several weeks and watch for small successes that bring YFT closer to the desired behavior. After trying a strategy for several weeks, reflect on what worked and what didn't. If your data isn't clear, keep collecting it for another week. Relationships and behavior changes take time and patience to develop and grow.

- *Examine your privilege*: Educators need to talk about and examine their own privileges throughout the year (Social Justice Tool Box, n.d.). As a white educator, I need to constantly consider that students of color and students furthest from educational justice may face things that I never imagined as a child— intergenerational trauma, racism, implicit bias, economic challenges, food security, and much more. Using discussion tools, like Social Justice Tool Box, can guide educators, especially white educators, through these important discussions. This is essential work to ensure we are building and sustaining a safe learning environment for YFT.

- *Check yourself*: Teaching takes a ton of physiological and mental energy. Your students need you to walk into your classroom with a positive mindset every day. When you are feeling tired or overwhelmed, you may need to take a deep breath, step back and reflect, or give yourself a moment to refresh yourself. If you are feeling slammed, take a personal day to regroup. Your Finest Teacher needs you to bring your best self to your classroom daily.

- *What you feed will grow*: Reinforcing desired behavior and striving to ignore undesired behavior whenever possible is the key to success for YFT.

As educators, it is up to us to change. We need to be patient and give grace to ourselves as well as YFT and celebrate each small step up the Learning to Read Hill. Building belonging and helping to accelerate learning momentum for every student is a profound professional gift.

Chapter 7: Momentum Checklist

Reflect: Think about your relationship with YFT. Are connections established or are you still working on this? What is YFTs behavior telling *you*—are their needs getting met?

Assess: Student and family surveys can provide information on students' strengths, interests, and needs. One-on-one meetings with students are helpful for relationship building and coaching. Formative assessment reading data through a formal tool or ongoing running records helps monitor independent reading levels. Tools such as Positive Discipline's (n.d.) Mistaken Goal Chart and Greene's (2020) *Assessment of Lagging Skills and Unsolved Problems* can identify specific concepts to target. See also Nelsen (2006) and Greene (2014).

Plan: If you suspect student needs aren't getting met, try these ideas:

- *Frequent connections.* Individually check in with YFT at the start of the day, before transitions, after recess, after lunch, and at the end of the day. Talk about their interests, the weather, sports, whatever! The most important thing is relationship building.
- *2 By 10 check in.* A "2 ×10 check in" is a structure where a teacher "checks in" with a

student for two minutes each day for 10 days to build relationship. But don't stop after 10 days! This is an essential daily practice with our YFTs, and joyful for you and them.

- *Schedule lunch together.* Schedule a time to eat lunch with Your Finest Teacher. Talk about their interests and passions. Try to find a particular area of interest that you can support and celebrate, such as rooting for the same team or finding library books on a specific topic.
- *Start a club.* Lunchtime clubs are powerful vehicles for strengthening belonging and fostering a student's passion.

Do: Put your plan into action and monitor how it is going. Refine your systems to meet YFTs emerging needs and your needs as you design efficient, equity-centered systems. Implement strategies to strengthen interpersonal and instructional belongingness for YFT.

Momentum Checklist

☐ *Reflect*

☐ *Assess*

☐ *Plan*

☐ *Do*

Chapter 8

The Power of Professional Partnerships

"Alone we can do so little,
together we can do so much."

—Helen Keller, American author, lecturer, political activist

"Never doubt that a small group of thoughtful,
committed citizens can change the world; indeed, it's the
only thing that ever has."

—Margaret Mead, American cultural anthropologist

As a beginning teacher, I learned the hard way to handle student problems on my own rather than come to my new principal with any issue—she was explicit about it. I learned the hard way not to ask my experienced colleague if I could borrow an extra textbook from her class—those school-purchased textbooks remained in her class for her students. I learned the hard way not to sit in "that chair" in the staff room—Mr. Jones always sat in "that chair" at lunch. The school's many unwritten rules and hidden agendas were stifling forces.

In contrast, my next teaching position was at a brand-new school with visionary school leader Principal Trevor Calkins. He established that a key pillar of our innovative school would be collaborative partnerships between staff members. Initial teacher applicants were invited to apply with a partner, so I applied with my best friend, Marjorie Roach. Time for collaborative planning and professional development was built into the weekly schedule, which communicated that teamwork was valued and made a difference in student learning. Teachers were encouraged and supported when they collaboratively led schoolwide initiatives, such as reading events, environmental stewardship initiatives, and musical performances. These powerful professional partnerships were invaluable as I learned from my colleagues and with my colleagues and cultivated my professional joy. When I became a school principal, I brought these same partnership systems and strategies to my schools, as I had joyfully experienced the power of professional partnerships.

Partnerships Are a Cornerstone of Learning

Partnering with other humans, both colleagues and families, make each of us a more effective educator. While families are a child's first partners in learning, teachers become crucial learning partners in developing skills and empowering achievement. Collaborative partnerships empower educators. Just like students, educators are fueled by feeling a sense of belongingness in their schools, which in turn improves skills and learner achievement.

Partnerships Are Assets to a School Community

Hargreaves and Fullan (2012) used a business model to identify "capital" as anything that adds value to an organization. Their research identified three ways that partnerships are assets that are beneficial within a school community: human, decisional, and social capital.

- *Human capital* is the talent, ability, and skills of the school's staff. The impact that each human brings to the collective staff places a crucial weight on the principal's and district's equitable hiring practices. There needs to be a racially balanced educator cadre at every school who brings their individual and group "be the change" commitment to critically examine, refine, and create equity-centered systems with social justice and culturally responsive foundations.

191

- *Decisional capital* is the ability of teachers and administrators to individually and collectively make effective judgments about student work, specific incidents, and managing and leading teams. Decisional capital improves over time as we strengthen our relationships and establish equity-centered systems and schedules that make time for collaboration.

- *Social capital* is how teachers and principals collaborate in a supportive culture. In a school, social capital is ever-changing, so it needs the regular attention of every principal, assistant principal, and teacher throughout the year. Each teacher brings their own ideas for how they can impact the ecosystem of their school environment. At the same time, when personal and professional challenges impact one staff member, this impact can ripple throughout a staff.

The impact of social capital may be magnified for educators of color because their feelings of safety, belonging, and trust can be affected by the ongoing missteps, microaggressions, and biases of others. The ongoing caste-based structures that continue throughout North American society require explicit intervention and ongoing facilitation so that historic racist practices can be eliminated individually, collectively, and systemically (Wilkerson 2020). It takes time, education, and determination to wipe out ignorance, address anti-Blackness, and tear out systemic racism so that we can have welcoming learning communities for all students, families, and staff.

Partnerships Generate Belonging

Learning can only begin once relationships are established. Whether we are in classrooms or staff rooms, we all need to feel safe through belonging and trust. Teaching is a highly isolating profession, so it is essential that principals and assistant principals establish schoolwide practices for welcoming new staff, sharing, and helping to navigate the expectations and norms—as well as traverse any unhelpful unwritten rules of each building. I've been blessed to learn from many incredible principals who welcomed new ideas, modeled the power of collaboration, encouraged innovative practices, and supported staff to organize social gatherings that were welcoming, inclusive, and fun. Onboarding new staff, creating schedules that provide time for collaboration, and supporting staff to implement innovative, equity-centered initiatives that improve student learning are essential responsibilities for school leaders.

Human capital needs to be nourished. "Parallel play" is the traditional side-by-side existence where teachers and principals keep to their own classrooms and offices; this was the environment I began my career in. Opportunities for collaboration need to be calendarized, supported, and refined throughout the year.

Drago-Severson's (2009) research found that within a staff, there are three types of professional relationships: adversarial, congenial, and collegial:

- *Adversarial relationships* are competitive and lack a respectful exchange of ideas; these relationships are toxic as the ripples of disgruntlement and disagreement swell and surge through a staff.

- *Congenial relationships* are positive social interactions between staff but are not necessarily focused on learning; these are the folks you say hi to in the staff room, but you don't know them well enough to go to them with a problem.

- *Collegial relationships*, or what I call collaborative partnerships, happen when teachers feel safe enough to go to a trusted colleague and/or administrator to discuss teaching practices, share knowledge, observe each other, and/or help each other out.

Schools need to establish structures that promote collaborative relationships. This happens when principals and staff intentionally build and refine relationships throughout the year. This happens when principals and teachers align their goals with school and district goals. And most importantly, this happens when time is built into the daily and weekly schedule for collaboration to highlight and honor this essential work.

Strategies for fostering collaborative professional partnerships include:

- Create a welcoming onboarding process with a Staff Handbook that outlines equity-driven school expectations, practices, and systems.

- Schedule time for one-on-one meetings with each new staff member.

195

- Explicitly state the school's values and expectations at the start of the year to communicate a professionally and personally supportive community.

- Because educators are in the business of helping humans learn, they need to be supported to "put on their own oxygen masks" before helping others, especially in times of personal crisis.

- Create an 'open door' policy, so staff collaboratively seek solutions together whenever a 'learning opportunity' (aka: a problem, mistake and/or shenanigan) arises.

- Share a wondering, observation, or insight about a student with a teacher to work together to support YFT.
- Build collaboration time into the school's weekly schedule and school calendar, so partnering is clearly valued as it is built into working hours.

Aligning Our Work on Our Mission, Vision, and Goals

When we are aligned our mission, vision, and goals, we can keep our purpose visible to everyone. For example, I post our three school goals at the top of every staff meeting and reference them in every PTA Principal Report. I reference these goals in staff weekly updates and school communications. I model embedding our school's goals into my own professional goals for my annual evaluation, and I invite teachers on staff to align their professional goals with the school goals, district goals, and my own professional goals, so we all have a unified, clear purpose for working together. I provide time for staff professional learning networks and grade group teams to work together on our aligned goals. During our work together, each of us constantly reflects and refines our work to continuously impact the ecosystems of our school community. Aligning my goals with individual teacher goals, grade group team goals, and district goals ensure we are all focused on the same mission and vision. This common purpose becomes a unifying element in our collaborative work.

"Be the Change You Want to See in the World"[16]

Each educator has the power to bring positive change to their classroom, their school, and their district. Teachers, school leaders, and district leaders impact the change in the ecosystems of our learning communities. Whether you share

---

[16] This quote has been attributed to Mahatma Gandhi for many years. Alas, this is incorrect. See Ranseth (2015).

what you learned from a podcast in the lunchroom with colleagues, encourage your team to diversify who they are following on social media, start a book club, sign up for a webinar, join a committee, or speak up in a staff meeting, your voice matters! Reflect thoughtfully on plans and actions to bring equity-driven change individually and collectively to systems.

An example of systemic change took place in Seattle Public Schools, led by Assistant Superintendent of Academics Dr. Keisha Scarlett, leader of the school district's 2019 Equity, Partnerships, and Engagement Division. Scarlett focused on innovative problem solving to elevate promising practices and build the capacity of adults to guide organizational development throughout the system (Seattle Public Schools, n.d.). Under Dr. Scarlett's leadership, this inspiring team of brilliant educators implemented equity-centered systems and practices that supported students across the district as well as students in the district's Schools of Promise. Their focus built individual student momentum and collective school momentum through system change.

Dr. DeLeon Gray (2021) wisely states that each educator contributes knowledge, information, and experiences to our schools, and this, in turn, makes our schools and our district stronger. Equity-driven educators have the power to actively shape what the system looks like for today's educators and for educators in the future. Gray notes, "Part of an equitable ecosystem involves creating and contributing to a sense of community among educators within the system." Teachers and school leaders must create and/or seek out opportunities for themselves to strengthen our professional belonging within our schools and our district. Our professional belongingness benefits ourselves and, in turn, benefits our educational ecosystems in progressive ways. Educators actively shape what today's educational systems look like as we socialize new equity-centered teachers into the system. Diversity and inclusion add enormous value to educational systems and benefit every student, family, teacher, and school leader. This, in turn, benefits the district as a whole. When learning ecosystems grow and evolve into more equity-focused and progressive ways of doing things, this transforms the system into the change we want to see in the world.

Systemic Structures:
Making Time for Collaboration

Hargreaves and Fullan's (2012) research supports the powerful impact of staff collaboration on achievement. When staff enjoy and value their collaborative work together, this improves both student learning and adult learning. In his and John McCarthy's national study on collaboration in public schools, Rutgers Professor Saul Rubinstein reported ". . . we see significant and important gains for students when there is greater collaboration" (McCarthy and Rubinstein 2017). The more teachers have time built into their schedules for collaboration, the greater the chance that colleagues will learn and grow together, which promotes belonging and trust and ultimately results in academic achievement and job satisfaction.

Several systemic structures can foster and support collaboration.

Collaborative Meetings: Explicit time should be built into the weekly schedule for collaboration. Teachers and I created a weekly meeting time that teachers could book if they wanted to get input from colleagues to generate or refine strategies for YFT, identify data to gather to learn more about YFT or organize additional services. This weekly Collaboration Meeting timeslot brings teachers, other classroom teachers, and specialists together to collegially brainstorm the next steps. Putting our heads together works! Frankly, the ideas we create together are far superior to anything we would have individually come up with on our own. Each meeting ends with the next steps, and we book a follow-up meeting on the spot so the teacher walks out with an intervention plan and feels supported. Collaboration is powerful, as it makes a difference in student learning and equity-centered practices.

Staff Meetings: Efficient, effective staff meetings maximize collaborative time and minimize the boring but essential stuff. First, the power of any meeting is in collaborative discussions, so information items were relegated to printed news items at the end of the agenda. Second, meetings only happen if we have topics to discuss or solutions to seek; updates or "heads up" advisories are provided in e-mails or quick one-on-one conversations. Third, set a time for the discussion and identify a timekeeper to keep everyone on track. When staff knows that meetings are efficient, recognize the power of their collaborative voice, and feel that their valuable time is honored, this builds professional belongingness and trust, which increases productivity and job satisfaction.

Professional Development (PD) and Professional Learning Networks (PLN): These collaborative learning structures are crucial for individual and collective equity-driven professional growth. First and foremost, we are humans who need to feel safety, belonging, and trust before we can learn. Learning together can build collegial relationships, which can impact an educator's professional capacity to take risks and try new strategies, which in turn can impact student learning. Educational researcher Dr. Eleanor Drago-Severson's developmental model consciously cultivates teacher and principal capacity as learners (2009). Her research found that teaming, providing leadership roles, creating collegial inquiry, and mentoring support all adults, regardless of their experience or training. Mechanisms to implement this model include professional development (PD) and professional learning networks (PLNs).

Professional development is the educational system for teachers and/or principals to learn innovative practices, strategies, and structures. Historically, PD has been slow to catch up to educational research, so presenters droning on like the 1950s "sage on the stage" still sadly continue. Educators should no longer be learning in a "sit and git" model. Teachers and principals need to be engaged in new learning, just like students. Facilitators following a "guide on the side" or a "mentor at the center" model can create a feeling of belonging as they foster research-based learning concepts and discussions to take place. When professional development is interactive and infused with collaboration opportunities, it can be inspirational, highly galvanizing, memorable, and fun!

Professional learning networks or professional learning communities (PLCs) are teams of educators who learn and collaborate on a common topic. PLNs and PLCs are research-based structures that improve instruction (Prenger et al., 2020). They can be staff-based, specialty-based, or district-based. PD, PLNs, and PLCs are most powerful when they are aligned with school goals and focus on research-based practices, and time is built into the school schedule for them to happen during work hours. Facilitators need to align their work with brain science so that participants remain engaged, focused, and productive, especially after just finishing a full day of teaching. Aligned PD, PLNs, and PLCs are the cornerstone for implementing research-based teaching practices to continuously support adult learning that enhances individual capacities, student success, and school improvement.

PLNs and PLCs are where the collaborative magic happens. By building relational trust, educators can shift from collegial relationships to collaborative partnerships where authentic teaming can take place. PLNs and PLCs attract teachers with common interests, but it is the collegial relationships that make it safe to discuss practices, share knowledge, and help one another.

Leadership Opportunities Honor Brilliance and Share the Load: Leadership roles offer teachers the opportunity to focus on their passion-focused initiatives in each school. Whether leading collegial inquiry or mentoring colleagues, taking on a leadership role allows teachers and principals to learn and grow together as they increase their individual and collective capacity for innovative instructional practices. For example, a teacher notices a student struggling and, after partnering with parents, tries three different strategies. The student continues to struggle and, in addition, becomes anxious and frustrated. So, what's next? At my current school, staff has several options: They can turn to their grade group team partner, as there is regular time in our schedule for teachers to have these collaborative discussions. They can meet with a Teacher Leader and/or schedule an observation in a colleague's class. They can turn to anyone on staff, including me, as a thought partner so we can strategize together. They can partner with families. Or they can book a time to meet with our school's Multi-Tiered Systems of Support (MTSS) team for a collaborative meeting. Multiple collaborative opportunities foster an equity-centered educational ecosystem that shares the load, empowers educators and students alike, and propels the learning community to support every child while getting better along the way.

Sharing the load also includes staff committees. Sharing responsibilities to plan an initiative or event, analyze data, or implement innovation is efficient and effective. For example, our school's MTSS team analyzes ongoing student reading data and reports our progress for our students at staff meetings so we can all collaborate on how we can continuously improve. Time is allocated in staff meetings for this important discussion. The school schedule is organized, so teachers have regular time for connecting with colleagues during their preparation time and regular time with grade group teams to align equity-driven planning, teaching, and initiatives.

Teacher momentum is just as important as student momentum. Building and sustaining professional partnerships is essential to work, as educators must feel safe and have a sense of belonging with the staff so they can create welcoming environments for students. Establishing interpersonal belonging on staff lays the foundation for creating effective instructional belongingness as teachers. Staff and administrators learning together through PD, PLNs, PLCs, and collaborative meetings exponentially improve the educational ecosystem of the school and the district. Ultimately, collaborative work results in institutional belongingness, which empowers effective teaching and learning. Teachers and principals need to feel energized and empowered to help every learner, and this physiological, emotional, and social momentum comes from the collaborative partnerships we form with colleagues and parents. Collaboration is where the magic happens, as it is by working together that the endorphins flow, our collective energy picks up, and the learning magic happens for students. Cultivate your professional joy through helping children learn and from the collaborative relationships we form to support one another to thrive in our learning communities.

Case Studies

First Grader Luis's teacher, *Ms. Acquin*, was an enthusiastic first-year teacher who embraced teaching her class with passion and determination. Through her ongoing assessments, she observed that multilingual Luis wasn't yet meeting expectations in reading. She wasn't sure how to start, and as a beginning teacher on new staff, she didn't yet have relationships with her new colleagues to easily reach out to. With her Fall Reading Assessments in hand, Ms. Acquin talked with her experienced grade group team partners to identify additional strategies to support Luis, a beginner in reading. They recommended that she meet with Luis' parents to identify Luis' strengths, interests, and needs to learn what the family saw at home. She worked with our school's Reading Specialist, who shared additional English language learner (ELL) differentiation strategies and provided Tier II reading support. She joined our school's Reading PLN and began implementing research-based strategies to increase multilingual Luis' feelings of interpersonal and instructional belonging. Ms. Acquin tracked Luis's reading progress through running records and saw that he was showing some growth but wondered if there were additional strategies she could try. She came to our school-based collaborative meeting, where we brainstormed further ideas; at the end of the meeting, she reported that one of her takeaways was that she felt both professionally supported and reassured that her interventions were research-based. By the next collaborative meeting and the next Parent–Teacher Meeting, she shared running record data on Luis's consistent reading progress and celebrated that he was ready to transition out of Tier II reading support by year-end.

Second-Grader Sophie's teacher, experienced *Mr. Valencia*, used regular running records to monitor new-to-the-school Sophie's progress in reading. He was concerned about her reading avoidance at school and at home, so he increased his in-class support for her through small, guided reading groups and frequent individual connections. As well as meeting with Sophie's Mom, Mr. Valencia also phoned Sophie's First Grade teacher at her previous school to identify her strengths, needs, and interests. Mr. Valencia worked closely with his grade group team and teacher leaders to partner on supporting Sophie. He collaborated with long-time teaching colleagues to team-teach a guided reading lesson together to expand their instructional strategies. Through this collaboration, Mr. Valencia reached out to Ms. Acquin to share what was working for Sophie to see if these same strategies would help Luis. As an experienced teacher working on a collaborative staff, Mr. Valencia felt supported by colleagues, so it felt professionally safe for him to ask questions and alter his practices to meet Sophie's needs, and in turn, he felt comfortable partnering with his new colleague, Ms. Acquin. Collaborating with colleagues provided additional information, energy, and partnership to support Mr. Valencia's ongoing efforts to help Sophie. By the end of the year, Sophie was reading at grade level, and Mr. Valencia, his colleagues, and Sophie's mom enthusiastically celebrated her successes together. Mr. Valencia brought his professional experiences to meet the needs of his current and future learners and simultaneously cultivated his professional joy.

Chapter 8: Momentum Checklist

Reflect: As an educator, what have your professional experiences been like on different staffs? Identify what worked and what didn't work for you. Keep this knowledge of your professional learning needs in your mind and your heart as you plan next steps.

Assess: Review YFT data. Do you have multiple professional avenues to follow when you seek new ideas and new ways of doing things? Do you have colleagues who can support you, either informally or formally, as you support YFT?

Plan: Identify a trusted colleague and make a plan to reach out for informal collaboration sessions. Partner with the adults who can support YFT: teacher, family, administrator, and so on. Work as a partnership team to more closely focus on the areas that will build YFT's momentum.

Do: Implement your plan for your professional partnerships. Putting this into action means building in time in your schedule so that collaboration is infused into your professional practice. Build time into your day to connect with colleagues on a collegial level to set the tone for safe collaboration opportunities.

Momentum Checklist

☐ *Reflect*

☐ *Assess*

☐ *Plan*

☐ *Do*

Chapter 9

The Power of Parent Partnerships

*Parents need to know that you are teaching their child,
not the curriculum.*

—Anita Koyier-Mwamba,
Seattle Public Schools Project-Program Manager

Look . . . with eyes of love.

—Dr. Keisha Scarlett,
Seattle Public Schools Assistant Superintendent
of Academics – Chief Academic Officer

As a kid, my concept of parental involvement in my
school was my mom baking cupcakes for the school bake
sale. Looking back, I think my mom was expected to be seen
and not heard. By the time our own children entered school,
my husband and I were keen to follow the conventional
practices of the day to support our children's learning: we
diligently listened to each child read nightly for their Home–
School Reading Program, played math card games to
practice multiplication facts, attended Parent–Teacher
Conferences, and volunteered at the Spring Fair. Our
assistance was valued, but it wasn't necessarily a
partnership. It wasn't until I was a middle school principal

211

that I woke up to the true power of authentically partnering with families, as staff, families, and I collaboratively

re-envisioned, reorganized, and renamed our school to become the first public global middle school in Canada. It was this genuine home–school collaboration that opened my eyes and broadened my horizons to see the true potential for students when educators authentically work with families.

Family Partnerships Build and Sustain Momentum

To learn, students must feel safe enough to take learning risks. When students feel belonging, safety, and trust at school, they will be successful (Gray et al. 2018). To be successful, students need to know that they, *and their families*, are safe, welcomed, and accepted. Teachers and school principals need to establish a partnership with families, as the family is the expert on their child. The bottom line, if students think that their family trusts you, then they will trust you. When trust is built between home and school, then students will start moving forward and keep moving forward. Family partnerships build and sustain momentum.

As the University of Washington Associate Professor Dr. Ann Ishimaru found "(p)olicymakers have long seen parents and families as key levers for improving U.S. student outcomes and success . . . ." (Ishimaru 2017). Schools partnering with families not only makes sense but is also essential. Ishimaru identified the importance of establishing equitable collaborations with families (Ishimaru 2020). Ishimaru's research found that schools should work closely with the people who know their children the best (Ishimaru 2014).

As educators partner with families to support learning for every student, school districts must ensure there are equitable means of engaging with parents as we shift from traditional "bake sale involvement" to working together as equal members. We need to *come together at the child's table* as families bring their expertise about their child, and teachers and administrators bring their professional knowledge and teaching experiences to support learners.

> Coming together at the child's table means the school must establish and refine practices to ensure they are equity-centered, valuing both families and professionals as we work together to generate and sustain momentum for every learner.

To effectively partner with families, schools must:

1. Create a welcoming environment for children and families
2. Build and sustain relationships with families by learning *from* families
3. Build community capacity by learning *with* families
4. Navigate student-learning opportunities together
5. Advocate for system wide equity-driven change

Create a Welcoming Environment for Children and Families

Based on a customer service model, it is the school's job to engage the family and build relationships to support student learning. In good times and bad, staff and parents need to keep coming to the table to help each learner grow. As families furthest from educational justice may arrive with past histories, trauma, and/or current family challenges that potentially impact a home-school relationship, it is the responsibility of principals and teachers to effectively connect with every family to collaboratively create goals that support every student.

Ishimaru outlined the intentional reconstructive work that must occur at the individual, organizational, and systemic levels to create a welcoming environment for families. She references the essential shift to equitable collaborations, which takes engagement, time, relationship building, and the establishment of equity initiatives to build the capacity for the dominant culture to equitably partner with nondominant culture (Ishimaru 2020).

Research on the power of creating a welcoming environment for children and families was examined in *We Dare Say, Love*, which explored the development and implementation of the African American Male Achievement initiative in the Oakland Unified School District (Nasir et al. 2018). Researchers followed a group of Black male educators who changed district policy and practice to create a learning experience for Black boys rooted in love. This model, in turn, informed Seattle Public Schools' 2019 launch of The Department of African American Male Achievement (AAMA). Led by Assistant Superintendent Dr. Mia Williams, this department is responsible for:

. . . ensuring the district has the culture, conditions, competencies, and community connections needed for all Black and African American boys and young male students to be successful. The Department of African American Male Achievement (AAMA) directly aligns with Seattle Excellence, the district's Strategic Plan . . . (which is) . . . the collective commitment to unapologetically support and serve students and families furthest from educational justice. (Seattle Public Schools, "Policy 0030")

As schools prepare to shift to building and rebuilding partnerships with families, Ishimaru explained that the process includes transforming power, building reciprocity and agency, and fostering collective capacity through collaboration (Ishimaru 2020).

Build and Sustain Relationships with Families by Learning *from* Families

> Building parent partnerships begins with relationships, relationships, relationships. Just as professional collaborations are founded on authentic relationships, so too are collaborative partnerships with families. Ishimaru's research confirms that equitable collaborations begin with parents and educators forming a coalition. (Ishimaru, 2020).

Some strategic opportunities include:

- *Start of the year events*, such as "Welcome to Kindergarten" initiatives, "Back to School" events, "Meet the Teacher Night," and "Curriculum Night," provide families the chance to meet teachers and learn about the school year ahead. Welcoming families to every learning community initiate those important conversations at the get-go to build relationships that will focus on the common goal of helping every learner become a successful reader.

216

- *Scheduled parent-teacher meetings*, such as Fall Parent–Teacher Conferences, Student-Led Conferences, and individual parent-teacher meetings, focus on the spectrum of students' academic, emotional, and social learning. Building and sustaining positive relationships with families helps cordial connections become collaborative partnerships as we seek solutions together for the sake of their child.

- *Ongoing communications*, such as class newsletters, school websites, and school newsletters, keep families informed about upcoming events and provide information throughout the school year. For equity's sake, communications need to be via multiple platforms (e-mails, text messages, and social media posts) to ensure accessibility for all families. These communications must also be provided in multiple languages to ensure multilingual families are informed in full.

Build Community Capacity by Learning *with* Families

For parents to support their child's learning, it is helpful to explain "the why behind the what" so families have the research and philosophy behind the school's curriculum choices, instructional practices, and research-based initiatives. Ishimaru (2017) identifies "parent capacity building" as an effective reciprocal relationship-building strategy. Individual families and Parent–Teacher Associations (PTAs) can deepen partnerships when families are authentic partners at the table with educators on school initiatives. At the same time, families have a myriad of experiences and perspectives, so family information sessions, PTA meetings, and individual home–school conversations can be challenging work, especially if parental philosophy differs from school or district philosophy. There are times when we need to agree to disagree. Listening, learning together, acknowledging common ground, and navigating the next steps are essential components of collaborating with families.

Pre-pandemic, I shared background information on school initiatives and upcoming events in newsletters, assemblies, and at PTA meetings. During the pandemic, parental requests for help exploded as they tried to support their child in remote learning! After surveying families in our school to find out what they needed during remote learning, I offered monthly, one-hour online *Family Partnership* webinars on topics they wanted, such as "Helping Children with Reading and Math" and "Talking with my child about race, racism, and anti-racism." I also became a co-facilitator in an accredited college course for parents and used the topics that my families requested as potential topics for course participants. When families could access information via multiple platforms, there was greater understanding and acceptance of initiatives. Families felt better prepared to support their children, and this helped students be successful. Our collaborative efforts empowered families to take an equitable seat on their child's learning team. Building parent capacity built our community's momentum.

Navigate Student Learning Opportunities Together

There are times when school and families need to come together responsively to support a student, whether the learner needs support for academic struggles, anxiety, frustration, anger, or sadness. If the teacher and principal have established a relationship with the family, the stage is set for everyone to deal compassionately with each learning opportunity together. If a strong relationship isn't in place yet, or if family and school disagree on how to handle it, sometimes things can get messy. But even in times of disagreement, it is essential to keep our shared goal of supporting the struggling student uppermost in mind.

Navigating learning opportunities together is at the heart of home–school partnerships. Sometimes these are after-school conversations with the teacher and parent when the teacher notices a child is struggling with something, has been hurt by another child's words or actions, or has harmed a classmate with words or actions. With a compassionate, equity-driven stance and an established relationship, adults can work together to help a child learn and grow. If academic, emotional, or social struggles continue, the teacher and family will likely meet to support the learner. If a student has been harmed physically or emotionally by another child's actions, then the coming to the table may include the counselor and/or principal. While we all may come to the table with different experiences and knowledge, it is up to educators to uphold the family's expertise about their child and constantly strengthen our individual and community capacity to uphold equitable, anti-racist actions. At the moment, it can compound the problem if teachers, principals, and/or families come to the table with viewpoints centered solely on the dominant culture or global minority, as this can get in the way of everyone feeling valued and understood at the table. Through ongoing professional development for global minority colleagues, principals and teachers need to lead courageous conversations so that North American educators pivot away from current systemic racism and emphatically shift to equity-centered practices with all families.

Mistakes and playground conflicts will happen daily. Humans will have disagreements, and sometimes young humans express their anxiety and anger by fight, flight, freezing, or fright. *It is essential to keep in mind that every problem, argument, shove, and shenanigan is a learning opportunity.* As a principal, it is my responsibility to partner with families to navigate conflicts so that children learn from them.

At the same time, as everyone comes to the table with different perspectives, lived experiences, potential intergenerational trauma, and presumptions, home–school partnerships can be messy at times. For nondominant families, this can be especially true, as they bring the added burden of systemic racism, implicit bias, and past microaggressions to the table. Educators must be mindful of the potential privilege, and power school staff bring to the table. Teachers and principals must strive to navigate differences and conflicts with empathy and compassion.

Advocate for Systemwide Equity-Driven Change

Families bring their children to schools with the hope and faith that their child will be taught according to state standards by an inspirational teacher who loves their child. Beyond clearly communicating the school's mission, vision, and goals, a principal needs to create buy-in within the learning community so that equity-centered school goals become *our* goals. Beyond teachers adopting the school's goals as their own professional goals, it's imperative that families adopt these same culturally responsive learning goals. Moving forward together for the sake of our learners is powerful for children when the adults in their lives are on the same page.

Ishimaru's research indicates that systemic collaboration is founded on multiorganizational educational equity initiatives like Seattle Public Schools' Equity Partnerships and Engagement Division and Schools of Promise. When School Partnership Manager Dr. Anita Koyier-Mwamba and Coordinator of School and Family Partnerships Asosa Sailiai supported schools to effectively build strong family partnerships, their efforts helped to improve student success and school culture through their advocacy for equitable family partnerships. Fostering collaborative home–school partnerships, through professional development, consultation, and coaching became essential components of building student and family belongingness and momentum.

Building partnerships happens when power and responsibility are shared between schools and families. This is a crucial and essential shift for schools.

Case Studies

As a new *First Grade teacher, Ms. Acquin* was initially reluctant to reach out to Luis's family with her concerns about his reading progress and his reading avoidance in class. She was not only new to teaching but new to the community and striving to build relationships with her students. In hindsight, she realized she wasted a lot of time focusing on what wasn't working with Luis rather than centering her differentiation strategies on Luis's strengths and interests. After she observed Luis and gathered data to share, she met with his family. She learned that they were very proud of his math and science achievement, and the family suggested incorporating culturally responsive nonfiction books into Luis's IDR at school and home. This equitable collaboration became a turning point, as Luis flourished when he was recognized as a science expert in class and thrived when he helped classmates in math. Ms. Acquin realized that two-way communication centered on sharing power and responsibility accelerated Luis's learning momentum. She vowed to initiate respectful family partnerships right from the start in the future.

At the beginning of the first full pandemic school year, *experienced teacher Mr. Valencia* reached out to every student's family by phone, e-mail, and/or in person. During his meeting with Third Grader Isabella's family, her parents shared their concerns about her reluctance to read at home. Mr. Valencia had taught Isabella's older sister two years beforehand and had helped the family successfully set up Home Reading at that time. As a home–school partnership had already been established, Isabella's family knew they could trust Mr. Valencia. They shared their concerns and ideas with him, identifying that Isabella loved cats and she loved reading books where she could see Brown girls like herself. Together, they determined that Isabella would love decodable "just right" books about cats and/or culturally responsive books to build reading skills and confidence. Mr. Valencia made this happen quickly, which began an ongoing home–school collaboration that supported Isabella's learning momentum.

Family partnerships are essential to build and sustain student learning momentum. As we shift to the next chapter on practice, it becomes even more apparent how crucial parental expertise and support become.

Chapter 9: Momentum Checklist

Reflect: Think about your own family's role in your education journey. Were they positively involved? Permissive? Overly intense? Check your privileges: what privileges did you enjoy during your learning journey? How do your own learning experiences impact your interactions with Your Finest Teacher's family? What are you looking for? How do you honor their expertise about their child? How do you need to reframe your own thinking to meet the needs of every student and family?

Assess: How are you supporting Your Finest Teacher through family partnerships? What are you doing to create a welcoming environment, establish two-way communication, facilitate respectful interactions, and share power and responsibility? Where are there spaces to improve?

Plan: What are your next steps to establish and/or further develop an equitable family partnership with YFT's family? What small and big steps can you take to build relationship, align your own goals with school goals, make time for collaborations, and responsibly handle learning opportunities together?

Do: What can *you* do to make a difference for YFT? How are *you* proactively building relationship? How are you coming to the table of every learner's team so that responsibilities and power are shared with families? How are you currently handling learning opportunities for students, and what do you intend to do so that you establish equity-driven, solution-seeking practices?

Momentum Checklist

☐ *Reflect*

☐ *Assess*

☐ *Plan*

☐ *Do*

Chapter 10

The Power of Practice

Champions keep playing until they get it right.

—Billie Jean King, American tennis superstar

The only way a kid is going to practice is if it's total fun for him . . . and it was for me.

—Wayne Gretzky, Canadian hockey superstar

For my ninth birthday, my parents gave me the gift of piano lessons. Initially, I was excited as I imagined myself skillfully entertaining crowds at Carnegie Hall, but once I began daily practicing, reality set in. My fantasies of becoming a famous concert pianist evaporated as I faced the initial tedium of practicing. Playing one note with one finger in my beginner's piano book seemed boring and useless, but I reluctantly persevered. Over time, my wonderful piano teacher introduced songs I recognized, and suddenly practicing seemed more purposeful and fun to me. Once I figured out how to play Top 10 hits on my own, I became joyfully persistent. While I never became a renowned pianist, I practiced enough to gain the rudimentary skills to feel competent and confident and have fun. The key was practice.

Practice is the secret momentum-building strategy for learning. Ask any athlete, musician, or chef: you get better at something by doing it over and over. For kids, whether they are learning to walk, tie their shoes, ride a bike, or how read, practice is the only way to get there. Whether a human dreams of being "pretty good" or an "expert" at anything, practice is crucial (Long 2016).

Practice is essential for both beginning bike riders and beginning readers. First-time bike riders are slow, wobbly, and fall down at first, but with trust and confidence, they are motivated to practice and take risks. Learning to read follows the same path as proficient bike riding. Self-confidence fuels motivation, which further builds mastery. Skills, motivation, and confidence exponentially fuel each other to propel learning momentum and achievement.

> Practice initiates and accelerates an interconnected physiological, emotional, and social process that leads to learning momentum.

Physiologically, practice fuels motivation and confidence because feeling confident actually accelerates learning. How does this work?

1. The amygdala, the brain's smoke detector, monitors emotions, survival instincts, and memory. When our ancient human ancestors spotted a saber-toothed tiger 300,000 years ago, their emotion (abject terror) was instantly connected to a fight/flight/freeze reaction. The amygdala keeps us alive by anchoring this experience (our feelings and fight or flight responses) to our memory—for next time!

2. When the amygdala smoke detector goes off, the hypothalamus determines what we apply to the fire. During a difficult task, if adrenaline courses through our body because we are angry or afraid, it is like applying gas to a fire. If we feel good about a situation, endorphins flow through our veins like water, helping us to stay alert, focused, and confident as we handle the job in front of us.

The more capable and confident our reader feels about the book they are reading, the better they can read it efficiently and effectively. Conversely, the more they want to avoid reading a complicated news article, the harder it will be. Fear and anxiety produce hormones that fan the flames of avoidance and anger.

Emotionally and socially, learners are motivated when they feel safety and trust in their classroom. Feeling connected to the teacher, classmates, and family has an emotional and social impact beyond the physical one. Not only do we want to fuel a learner's skills, but we also want to strengthen their confidence to help them physiologically increase their attention and focus on accelerating their productivity.

Our job as educators is to help a student systematically build reading skills. Just as practice improved my piano skills, daily reading is a key factor in improving reading skills, increasing feelings of competence, and ultimately accelerating motivation. In short, practice strengthens reading skills and exponentially accelerates proficiencies and confidence.

The Essential Components of Practice

To help learners get up the Learning to Read Hill, the effective practice involves setting an achievable goal, establishing routines, focusing, "just right" practice, recognizing the importance of struggle, and celebrating perseverance:

- *Begin with the end in mind:* Humans are innately goal driven to feel happy, competent, and in control and to help others (Hermans and Meijers 2019). Duckworth describes the importance of "deliberate practice" centered on a "stretch goal"

231

(Jacobson 2018). You don't spend hours learning to play the guitar for the sake of playing the guitar; you practice for hours to learn to play a song. Children are driven to tie their shoes because they want to be independent and/or be just like Big Sister. Students will persist with sounding out "c-a-t" because it feels good and/or makes them feel competent, and/or their ultimate goal is to read *The Cat in the Hat* on their own. Helping readers identify a clear goal, whether it is learning to read a specific book or joining classmates in discussing a series, can fuel a learner's desire to practice.

- *Establish reading routines:* Author Malcolm Gladwell (2008) said, "Practice isn't the thing you do when you are good. It is the thing you do that makes you good." In his book *Outliers,* he famously asserted that 10,000 hours of practice would make you an expert. Beginning readers need consistent practice to build their reading skills, as it takes mastery of discrete skills like decoding and comprehension as well as skill integration to become competent readers. This is hard work and takes time! It is essential to build daily routines for independent reading practice, as routines are essential components for developing new behaviors and skills (Ritchhart 2015). As *Atomic Habits* author James Clear (2018) reports, it takes many weeks to shift behavior from a task to a habit, so it is essential for beginning readers to have guided reading practice, phonics instruction, and daily independent reading practice. Establishing reading routines at school *and* at home further increases reading practice. It requires lots of encouragement and support from school and home to help a student get up the Learning to Read Hill, as this may be the very first time this young human repeatedly practices something that is hard and requires years to achieve mastery.

- *Focus:* What you pay attention to matters. Author Daniel Goleman (2013) zeroed in on the importance of maximizing attention and effort in his book *Focus.* Duckworth (2016) emphasized the importance of both *time-on-task* and *" high-quality" practice.* Just as I plunked, plunked, plunked away on the piano, or fell down for the umpteenth time on my bike as I learned to ride, I improved when I focused and persevered. An athlete must pay attention to specific elements of an effective throw, kick, or shot. Musicians must intentionally practice a difficult section repeatedly to refine their performance. Students must spend time intentionally practicing decoding, fluency, and comprehension, which empower them to learn to read.

- *"Just right" Practice*: Author Daniel Pink talks about finding the "sweet spot" when it comes to finding practice opportunities that are in the zone. He summarized the importance of this "just right" practice when he explained *"Goldilocks tasks"*:

  > *"If a task is too easy, people—whether they're children or adults—will get bored. If it's too hard, they'll get anxious or frustrated. You want that sweet spot, where something is within our range of challenge—not too easy, not too hard, but just challenging enough that we're engaged and being pushed to a slightly higher level. . . . We need to create more of those moments in school. If you're doing something easy, you're never going to improve; if you're doing something too hard,*

you're not going to succeed, so you won't improve that way either. But if you have a Goldilocks task, you're much more likely to move toward greater mastery." (Azzam 2014)

Children learning to read need practice with "just right" text. Developing readers need to be assigned "just right" texts so that their choice is which book they read first, not *if* they are going to practice reading, and then they can read their dessert books. This is when parent partnership becomes essential. Finding a book of interest that is also a "just right" text can be strengthened by a united home–school support system, so developing readers use their energy to build their skills and confidence through practice rather than expend their energy honing their skills in reading avoidance.

- *Struggle is essential for learning:* Jo Boaler (2016), Stanford professor and author of *Mathematical Mindsets,* says that ". . . if you aren't struggling, you aren't really learning" (Spector 2019). UCLA scientists Elizabeth and Robert Bjork talk about the importance of "desirable difficulties" as their research found that the brain needs to be pushed to do things that are hard (Bjork and Bjork, n.d.). We know that humans gravitate toward doing pleasurable tasks and avoid difficult ones. Because reading is a mentally taxing endeavor for beginning readers, they need adult support to work through the struggles of sounding out c-a-t to get to the joyful moments when they *can* independently devour Seuss' *The Cat in the Hat* and Litwin's *Pete the Cat.*

- *Celebrating perseverance:* Continuing to work hard despite adversity is the final key component of practice. Duckworth (2016) said, ". . . as much as talent counts, effort counts twice." Explicitly recognizing and celebrating hard work and determination can build and strengthen children's resolve to get up the Learning to Read Hill.

The Magic of Daily Reading

Learning to read takes practice. Educational researcher Richard Allington (1996) recommended students have a daily practice focused on time, text, and talk. A Home Reading program that complements effective literacy instruction focuses on:

- *Time:* For beginning readers, regular reading practice can start with about four to five minutes of Independent Daily Reading (IDR) four days a week, *based on the student's reading stamina.* (Gradually extend this to 15 to 20 minutes in Second Grade and 20 to 30 minutes in Third Grade.) Try setting a timer for a slightly shorter range to instigate IDR as a positive experience. Use a When/Then Model ("*When* you finish reading to me, *then* you can . . .") that rewards the child with an activity they can look forward to once they've accomplished the agreed-on IDR goal. This sets firm boundaries while helping young children keep moving forward at the end of the day. At home, families can establish specific days and times for Home Reading to anchor the routine; Monday through Thursday allows extra time for weekend relaxation. Partner with families to schedule Home Reading at a time that avoids arguments:

237

immediately after arriving home from school or immediately after dinner can sidestep initial transition conflicts. Aim for short and sweet with lots of encouragement to gradually build their stamina, reading skills, and confidence.

One promising practice shared by First Grade teacher Colleen Neves is scheduling time for re-reading last night's decodable "just right" Home Reading book to a classmate. This rereading gives extra practice and builds confidence.

• *Text:* Teachers and families can partner to identify "just right" texts and establish a system to exchange the books as children master them. For Kindergarten and First Grade students reading simple, decodable books, use the "Two Finger Rule": if a child stumbles/struggles/skips more than two words, the book is too hard. For Second and Third Graders, use the "Five Finger Rule": if they make more than five errors in 100 words, then the book is too hard. Follow guidelines for finding a book that is of interest and isn't too easy or too hard. For beginning readers, if a child is able to read a decodable book (a book that requires them to practice the phonemic sounds they are learning at school) for three nights in a row with confidence and no stumbling, they are ready to move on to a new book. As students gain experience and confidence, they will find authors and series they love to read, and this can propel them to read an entire series.

- *Talk*: As beginning readers practice Home Reading or extra-IDR-with-an-adult daily, it is an opportunity for adults to show full support and faith that YFT will learn to read. Establish a calm, consistent place to read, sit beside your young reader, encourage/commend them when they use their finger to "teach" their eyes to track, "notice" their perseverance, and reinforce when they go back and reread a tricky word, and cheer them on as they finish each book. One or two minutes of talk after they have read is also a crucial component, as it is this talk that reinforces the importance of comprehension. Canadian school leader, teacher, and University of Victoria Instructor Wendy Payne (2021) shared, "One of my favorite questions is 'Who would like this book? Why?' The key to *talk* is that we provide the student time to express their thoughts, and

239

teachers do more listening and encouraging than talking." What character did they like, why do they think that character was sad, and what would you have done if you were Little Red Riding Hood? Adult attention and enthusiasm will tip the scales toward reading independence.

The supportive practice that adults give to young learners is essential in a child's journey getting up the Learning to Read Hill. Whether we are teachers, family, or volunteers, we are essential facilitators to help children establish a reading practice routine to build their skills and confidence.

Back to My Finest Teachers ...

Luis's story highlighted the importance of parent partnerships, passion, and practice. When his family identified Luis's passion for math and science, his classroom teacher and I refocused on Luis's interests as we simultaneously partnered with his mom to establish a Home Reading program. The teacher ensured that Luis had culturally responsive books in his classroom, his Book Box, and his "just right" Home Reading books, as he thrived when he heard stories about his own culture and the cultures of others. The teacher helped Luis check out library books on rocks and snakes as his dessert books. Consequently, Luis became our First Grade resident math and science expert, reveling in sharing his science interests and helping classmates once he finished his tasks. By partnering with family and increasing practice, Luis began to see himself as a positive leader and helper in class. By the end of First Grade, Luis was meeting expectations in reading, math, and science, and he was a confident learner and leader in the class.

Chapter 10: Momentum Checklist

Reflect: What are you currently doing that is supporting YFT? Working from a strength-based model, identify YFT's strengths and interests that may help to foster and fuel their practice.

Assess: Using your ongoing data, record what is working and what is getting in the way. Talk with YFT to get their input as well, as *their* qualitative feedback is just as crucial as the qualitative data you are gathering.

Plan: Try to implement one strategy in Text/Time/Talk that will help *you* help them. Involving YFT in the plan will help them develop metacognitive awareness of their own learning and empower them to feel that they have voice and choice in this process. Help each learner be part of the solution.

Do: Plan to stick with this Text/Time/Talk strategy for one week before reviewing and refining. After one week, loop back to reflecting: what is working, what isn't working, and what you can do about it.

Momentum Checklist

☐ *Reflect*

☐ *Assess*

☐ *Plan*

☐ *Do*

Chapter 11

The Power of Passion

The new dawn blooms
As we free it.
For there is always light,
If only we're brave enough to see it.
If only we're brave enough to be it.

—Amanda Gorman, 2020 Inaugural Poet

When I was 10 years old, my family moved across town, and I started at a new school. While the relocation was exciting for my parents, I saw it as cataclysmic: the thought of being the new girl at a new school with kids I didn't know felt overwhelming. Luckily, my Fifth Grade teacher was Mr. Tom Heppell[17], an inspiring educator, skillful coach, and creative artisan, as he taught us to use pottery wheels to design coffee mugs that only a mother would love. Mr. Heppell noticed both my shyness and my love of reading, and he began to connect me with classmates based on our mutual love of books.

---

[17] Thank you to Mr. Tom Heppell's family for granting me permission to use his name posthumously.

Slowly but surely, I began to feel belonging and trust. At the same time, Principal Ken McCulloch[18], a larger-than-life entity, was a welcoming, inclusive school leader as he greeted students, staff, and families daily with enthusiasm and determination. When I became a teacher and then a school principal, I modeled myself after both wonderful educators who focused on relationships to create a warm, caring learning community.

In the spring of Fifth Grade, Mr. Heppell and Mr. McCulloch concocted a Fifth Grade enrichment initiative. Dividing our cohort into groups of five, they planned a weeklong, equity-centered enrichment activity for every group. For one week, four classmates and I were taken out of class to "work on a special project" with parent volunteers. Each group was pulled out of class (Yes! Pulled out of class!) to visit a local business and create a presentation to share what we learned. Our small group toured an orchid greenhouse that cultivated flowers for local florists. I didn't know anything about orchids or gardening, or running a business, but I loved developing our questions beforehand, interviewing the business owner, and then working together as a group to put our "report" together and prepare our presentation.

---

[18] Thank-you to Mr. Ken McCulloch's family for granting me permission to share this story posthumously.

Maya Angelou reminds us that people may not remember what you said, but they will remember how you made them feel! (Angelou 2003) I don't remember our report or our presentation, but I will always remember how I felt valued. This weeklong experience was transformational for me. Creating a unique learning opportunity for a group of young humans that allows them to feel special and collaboratively learn in a different way generated for me a lifetime of innovative ideas for empowering learners.

Throughout my career, my Fifth Grade "outside the box" project motivated me to create similar personalized empowerment initiatives for my students. A Passion Project is an umbrella term for any student-centered 'outside the box' initiative that empowers young humans to accelerate their learning momentum. First and foremost, a Passion Project builds momentum because helping kids feel special generates belonging and trust and can galvanize learners. Second, giving us the privileged opportunity to become orchid experts and business analysts whose voices, opinions, and actions mattered was an innovative, validating experience that helped me discover the power of student agency as it fueled my interpersonal and instructional belonging.

Passion Projects Galvanize Learning

Strengths, interests and hobbies motivate each of us to learn more and share our expertise with others. For students, one of the best ways to build their momentum is determine what they are excited about or good at, and provide the opportunity to share their learning or expertise with others.

After dreaming and scheming with colleagues, families, and students to identify a YFT's strength or area of interest, there are three models I've used in the past and continue to offer: clubs, leadership opportunities, and a individualized Passion Project designed specifically for a student's unique interests and needs. These initiatives are only limited by a child's imagination and the parameters of a school's schedule and budget.

Clubs: Gathering together to discuss a common interest or accomplish a shared goal strengthens belonging, build trust, fosters friendships, and can initiate activism for a lifetime. Clubs are student-driven, completely voluntary (students can drop in and drop out anytime), and are always, always, always inclusive (everyone is welcome to join any time). Ideas for clubs include:

- *Service clubs* focused on a common interest and/or services, such as the Green Team or the Gratitude Squad.

- *Student-initiated clubs* are group gatherings driven by students to discuss a common interest or accomplish a shared goal, such as Comic Book Club or organizing a Peace Walk. These clubs may last a while or fizzle after a few meetings, but no matter what, it brings kids together around common interests.

- *Adult-created clubs* are gatherings I create when I see a specific student who needs a belonging and/or empowerment opportunity or when there is a schoolwide need, fulfilled by starting a group such as Bulletin Board Design Team or School Museum for displaying student work.

Leadership Opportunities: As discussed in Chapter 6, service is a secret momentum-building strategy for establishing and strengthening belongingness (Gray 2021). Building on this fact, a leadership opportunity is any activity where a student can help others in a group setting and/or shine publicly. Opportunities can be centered around a learner's passions, such as starting a MakerSpace Club to work on crafts, creating a Joke Club to share riddles at lunch, or a middle school Book Club or high school Yearbook Committee. Or, a leadership opportunity can be in a service club setting, such as joining a Green Team to coordinate school-based composting, volunteering to be a Student Playground Coach at recess, organizing a Peace Walk, or preparing a Diwali Presentation for the school assembly. Whether these purposeful opportunities are student-driven or educator-initiated, they must give students agency to make an authentic difference in the world, whether it is school-based or in conjunction with a national organization like *Me to We.*[19] These types of leadership opportunities are also natural paths for students to collaborate with teachers and parents, further building on individual empowerment.

Passion Projects: If YFT needs to strengthen feelings of belonging and trust, is not able to find an existing school club that interests them, and/or is not excited about a leadership opportunity centered on their needs and interests, then it's time for a Passion Project—a powerful opportunity for YFTs to build self-confidence, belonging, trust, and learning momentum. Modeled after my own Fifth Grade "Outside the Box" Orchid Project, a Passion Project involves pulling them out of class for a short time, a block, or even a few days to focus on a topic that they are passionate about. This is absolutely academically driven, as they will likely do more research, reading, writing, listening, and speaking about their Passion Project than they would normally do in a week. And the knowledge they experience about themselves

---

[19] WE.org is a Canadian-based organization that works with K–12 students to promote human rights and social equality. For more information, go to: https://www.we.org/en-US/.

and the world will far exceed anything they or you could ever imagine.

The Passion Project may be patterned after a project-based learning initiative or a Genius Hour project, but it has a clear purpose: to make a difference in the world by informing or helping. Involving them in such an innovative initiative communicates to students that we care about them, that they have agency, and that they can make a difference in the world. This is all about the process for the student, but from my experience, the authentic final product is always mind-blowing. With a minimal time investment on the part of the educator, a game-changing opportunity can be created for a student, and their positive flourishing, in turn, impacts their own learning, their family, and our school community. That is what this is all about: *empowering humans to make a difference in the world is why we have schools.*

Every student deserves to feel as special as I did when I became an orchid expert for a week. Creating a Passion Project is one way to magnify and celebrate the unique gifts, strengths, and interests of each scholar. This can be a powerful pivot opportunity for Your Finest Teacher.

Four Steps to Creating a Passion Project

1. *Identify YFT:* As we identify YFTs at the start of each year, we also identify students who may have *actual needs* or *potential needs* during the year. An *actual needs* student exhibits a clear academic, emotional, or social need; they need help with learning, self-regulating emotions, and/or making friends. A *potential needs* student is a child you are keeping an eye on; they don't appear to have an imminent academic, social, or emotional need, but they may benefit from extra efforts to build belonging and trust. Or they may be a *leader-in-the-making* who would benefit from an opportunity to spearhead their great idea. All of these young humans would benefit from having something special in their lives. Whether they have *actual needs* or *potential needs,* each of these children becomes one of Your Finest Teachers.

2. *Gather and track data:* Data informs our practice and guides our work. Data may be academic or include teacher and parent observations, documented playground incidents, attendance, psychoeducational assessment, and so on. If there is a behavioral concern, it can help to have teachers complete a

screening tool, such as Greene's (2020) *Assessment of Lagging Skills & Unsolved Problems,* to identify a common, specific area to focus on as a Home–School Team. This data identifies a specific need and becomes the basis for documenting growth (see also Greene 2014).

3. *Collaboratively plan and personalize the passion project:* Once the YFT is identified and the necessary data is in hand, it is time for the Home–School Team to collaborate to personalize the project. There are three factors to consider:

   - *Align with YFT's strengths and interests:* Because strengths are a YFT's superpowers, identify the academic, emotional, or social skills that they can bring to the project. Hobbies and pursuits outside of school may be opportunities to explore. For example, if YFT loves to write, would the student like to be a reporter for the school newsletter? If the student loves to help others, could he assist once a week in a younger class as a Big Buddy or on the playground as a Student Playground Coach? If YFT likes to draw, could a lunchtime Drawing Club be created for YFT and peers? Next, consider the factors below.

- *Plan for time and space:* Passion projects can be during school time or outside of school time, such as right before/after school, during recess, or at lunchtime. If during school time, it should be aligned with learning standards so as not to detract from instructional time. A project can take place for a limited time, such as a short weekly stint as a 20-minute classroom helper in a younger class. Passion Projects need to be manageable for the adults involved, too—offer opportunities that are doable, positive for all students, and benefit YFT and classmates without inordinately impacting instructional time. (Keep in mind, it is totally valid to plan a differentiated "Special Project" during school time if it aligns with learning standards, such as reading, writing, listening, and speaking.) Space is also a consideration, as the Passion Project needs to be a supervised endeavor.

- *Set YFT up for success.* Since the purpose of the Passion Project is to build interpersonal and instructional belonging, adults need to be savvy about crafting the details of the project so that YFT feels successful without feeling overwhelmed or creating resentment from classmates. Put it in context: if YFT is alienating

253

peers because he is frequently trying out his karate moves aggressively while standing in line, then don't create a Karate Club. Otherwise, the project will further alienate peers while reinforcing unwanted behaviors. If all YFT wants to talk about is playing a violent video game at home that you know peers are not allowed to play, then you want to design a Passion Project that focuses on topics that will increase confidence and strengthen friendships without perpetuating the divide. Creating opportunities where YFT can work on the project with a friend or offer it as a club or volunteer opportunity to all may be ways to "build up" YFT in a positive light in front of peers. It is essential to set up YFT for success without alienating the student from peers.

4. *Implement, track, refine, and celebrate.* Once the Home–School Team has developed a potential Personalized Empowerment Project idea or ideas, strategize on how to present the proposal to YFT. Teachers and family can work together on the who, when, where, and how of making the pitch in a way that sounds like an exciting opportunity. Depending on the student, it might be more successful in having

a parent float the idea in advance of the teacher bringing it up, and in other cases, it works better if the teacher makes the suggestion and invites YFT to discuss the idea at home.

When planning the pitch, the adults also need to think about setting YFT up for success while considering autonomy and choice. Choices such as time and space need to be adult-determined, but if YFT rejects the opportunity outright, then it is back to the drawing board. Keep in mind this isn't a total failure if YFT declines the first suggestion because it communicates to YFT that educators care *and* also respect YFT's interests. Once underway, monitor how it goes for YFT. Support the student so that they feel successful, whether they decide to finish it or not. For Personalized Passion Projects, it is all about the journey, not the destination. If YFT loses interest and/or wants to focus on something else, let it go; a Passion Project is meant to be a benefit rather than a burden. Verbally reinforce when you notice that YFT is having fun, connecting with peers, and/or accomplishing their goals.

While setting this up takes time and energy, keep in mind that it is *far more effective and satisfying* to chat with a child over lunch about their baseball card collection, debate how their favorite football team will fare on Monday night, or discuss their favorite comic book series rather than calling a family to discuss the umpteenth fight they got into on the playground. Making Passion Projects come to life is a far preferred investment of our time and energy.

Whether you are creating a club, setting up a leadership opportunity, or crafting a Passion Project, creating Personalized Empowerment Projects is a gratifying, fun part of my job. Every human loves to talk about their interests. Families are thrilled to talk about their child's strengths. Teachers love to find out interesting things about their students and love to focus on positive, productive collaborations. School leaders revel in sharing impactful ideas that save time, avoid conflicts, and seek solutions. *Educators and families want to see students empowered to make a difference in the world.* This is a win for the kid, a win for their family, a win for educators, and a win for the global community.

An empowered kid is going to feel interpersonal belonging and trust. An empowered kid will be more confident than they were before. With endorphins flowing through their veins and trust starting to grow in their heart, the student will feel it is safe to take a risk in class and try. After being asked to help set up a club or join a project, YFTs will know what determination and perseverance feel like, they will feel empowered by their student agency, and this will fuel their learning momentum. With learning momentum underway, they will build their skills and their confidence.

Start looking around your school—you have future leaders awaiting your encouragement, experts waiting to be discovered, and Student Playground Coaches waiting in the wings. All they need is a little bit of encouragement and support from you. They need our love and imagination to build their learning momentum.

Back to My Finest Teachers . . .

- *First Grade soccer enthusiast and confident learner Malik* returned to in-person learning in Spring 2021 with continued determination. At our weekly whole school online assembly, he gave a presentation to share how he and his family celebrated Kwanzaa. He continues to exceed expectations in reading.

- *First Grade math and science enthusiast Luis* was motivated to read during IDR so he could be a Math Helper and Science Expert in class, assisting his peers after he finished his STEM tasks. Whether learning remotely or eventually

257

returning to in-person learning, Luis continues to meet expectations in reading.

- *Second Grade artist Sophie* helped me create a lunchtime Drawing Club and invited peers. This 30-minute online club provided a welcomed social interaction opportunity for young artists (and me!) during the pandemic. While interest eventually fizzled out, this positive social interaction allowed Sophie to connect with peers, practice her social skills, and strengthen her confidence. Increased confidence resulted in Sophie's increased willingness to practice reading at home. By the time we returned to in-person learning, Second Grader Sophie was meeting expectations in reading. Now in Third Grade, she is exceeding expectations in reading.

- *Third Grade Student Playground Coach Isabella*'s increasing confidence and practice had a powerful impact on her belonging and, ultimately, her reading skills. Ongoing collaboration between teachers and the established home–school partnership became essential at the start of the pandemic, as Isabella initially struggled emotionally, socially, and academically. Teachers continued working together to refine culturally responsive practices to meet Isabella's needs and the needs of all students, especially for students furthest from educational justice. Isabella's family and teachers continued partnering with perseverance to get Isabella back on track by fostering a relationship. Consequently, Isabella resumed her learning momentum. By the end of Third Grade, she was meeting expectations in reading based on an individual reading assessment conducted by the teacher.

Chapter 11: Momentum Checklist

Reflect: Think about your YFT observations and growth throughout the school year. Continue strengthening your relationship with YFT and their family every day. Continue observing—what do you notice in class, see on the playground, or surreptitiously catch in the hall? Your daily connections matter!

Assess: As you've worked throughout the school year to identify YFT's strengths, needs, and interests, continuously review and refine your target and your ideas. Do you want to build confidence by creating a project based on their strengths? Do you want to shape an initiative to help meet their needs of belongingness and trust? Do you want to craft a project around their interests?

Plan: As you plan a Personalized Empowerment Project, what are your parameters and logistics? Will a leadership opportunity take place in class time or outside of class? Who can you partner with to help make this opportunity happen? Is it driven by a timeline to create a product, or is it open-ended? If there are costs involved, make sure you determine funding sources before talking with the student. When you approach the child with an idea or possibility, you need to make sure you can deliver before you even begin the conversation. Figure out logistics in advance so that you know what choices you can offer the student.

Do: Communicate regularly with student, staff, and family before, during, and after this initiative. It is through authentic conversations with your Chess Club Coordinator, Playground Coach, Green Team Lead, or School Museum Designer that the trust is built, the relationship is strengthened, the confidence is fostered, and the magic happens. Plan for how you will recognize and continuously celebrate the student's growing persistence, determination, confidence, skills, and, ultimately, their learning momentum. Bottom line, YFT needs your love and support. They will have ups and downs, but celebrate who they are and their every tiny step forward. Empowerment is what fuels joy, strengthens determination, and drives our momentum forward.

Momentum Checklist

☐ *Reflect*

☐ *Assess*

☐ *Plan*

☐ *Do*

Chapter 12

Weaving It All Together

Stay focused, go after your dreams, and keep moving toward your goals.

—LL Cool J, American rapper, songwriter, record producer, and actor

There are many moving parts in life and many potential life pivots still to come for you, me, and educators everywhere. One thing is for sure—educators and families have a symbiotic relationship. Society depends on educators to lead the way in partnering with all families to help all families, especially those furthest from educational justice. As Canada's 2015 Truth and Reconciliation Commission Chairman, The Honorable Senator Murray Sinclair (2015) said, *"Education is the key to reconciliation . . . Education got us into this mess, education will get us out of it."*

The concepts put forth in this book are not new. The importance of every child learning to read by the end of Third Grade is well-established in educational research. Partnering with parents, using passion and purpose to fuel focus, and the importance of practice are all well-proven in scientific research.

Empowering Students Maximizes Student Learning Momentum: Implementing the research-based concepts of building belonging, balanced literacy instruction, deliberate practice with "just right" texts, and creating student-agency-driven Passion Projects *in unison* maximizes learning momentum to help children learn to read.

Partnerships Empower Student and Adult Momentum: Research shows there is a supplementary positive impact on belonging for families and educators when they collaboratively partner to support each child. Whether we are in regular school or a pandemic-era time of learning, student success empowers families, teachers, and school leaders, cultivating joy for all of us.

Practice Improves Reading: Research has taught us that we get better at things when we practice. Building IDR into daily school and home schedules improve reading skills, motivation, and confidence.

> Creating opportunities for belonging interpersonally, instructionally, and systemically deconstructs systemic racism and fuels learning momentum.

There is a powerful impact on school communities and cultures when families and educators partner to build learning momentum. Implementing Three Momentum Moves not only makes a difference for kids and adults but also positively transforms our educational systems.

As educators, whether ongoing societal storms or looking to ever-evolving educational research, we must continue to look to the future and apply our ongoing learning to our work in the future. We can no longer work in isolation; educators and families must partner on student learning. We can no longer ignore the passions of students; we must honor their inherent agency by incorporating their strengths and interests into the learning process. And families and educators must partner on the crucial elements of practice like never before so that student learning is solidly research-based, equity-centered, student-focused, and fueled by their own momentum.

What I Know for Sure

During the writing of this book, my first grandchild was born. Henry has grown from a tiny infant to a curious young human who is chattering enthusiastically, singing joyfully, dancing with savvy, and playing with others. He has books he loves and listens to every day. For me, he is the promise of a future of possibilities.

My personal and professional goal is to help every child to be a determined, perseverant, resilient human who understands that compassion, caring, and social justice must fuel our passion, partnerships, and practice every day.

Empowering children to become lifelong learners and confident readers happens when we love them every day, when we work together to build belonging and trust, when we identify a child's strengths and needs and help them build their learning momentum to ascend the Learning to Read Hill, when we fuel their passion and reinforce their reading skills through practice. When each small step is celebrated together with teacher and family support, together, we can help every learner overcome challenges as they build their "reading muscles" along with their perseverance, courage, and resiliency.

For my part, I will continue to love, watch, support, and empower every child's learning momentum. I am blessed to learn from and grow alongside My Finest Teachers every day as each student's learning momentum fuels my own momentum. Making a difference for learners and their families is what schools should be all about.

Bibliography

Momentum Bibliography is divided into 3 sections:

- References for all footnoted sources.
- Books on how to *actually* teach reading
- Children's books referenced within *Momentum.*

References

ACLU (American Civil Liberties Union). n.d. "School-to-Prison Pipeline." Juvenile Justice. https://www.aclu.org/issues/juvenile-justice/school-prison-pipeline.

Adler, Alfred. (1937). *Understanding Human Nature: The Psychology of Personality.* New York: General Press.

Aguilar, Elena. 2013. *The Art of Coaching: Effective Strategies for School Transformation.* New Jersey: John Wiley & Sons.

———. 2018. *Onward: Cultivating Emotional Resilience in Educators.* New Jersey: John Wiley & Sons.

Aguilar, Elena, and Lori Cohen. 2022. *The PD Book: 7 Habits That Transform Professional Development.* Hoboken, New Jersey: John Wiley & Sons.

Allington, Richard L. 1996. (Reposted 1/2/2018.) "The Six Ts of Effective Elementary Literacy Instruction." Washington: AdLit.Org. https://www.staffordschools.net/site/handlers/filedownload.ashx?moduleinstanceid=3573&dataid=49014&FileName=

The%20Six%20Ts%20of%20Effective%20Elementary%20
Literacy%20Instruction%20Reading%20Rockets.pdf.

———. 2011. *What Really Matters for Struggling
Readers: Designing Research-Based Programs*, 3rd ed.
Boston: Pearson.

American Institutes for Research. 2020. Reading and
Literacy. https://www.air.org/our-work/education/reading-
and-literacy.

Angelou, Maya. 1969. *I Know Why the Caged Bird Sings.*
New York: Random House.

———.*Conversations with Maya Angelou.*

Annie E. Casey Foundation. 2010. "Early Warning! Why
Reading by the End of Third Grade Matters*."*
https://www.aecf.org/resources/early-warning-why-
reading-by-the-end-of-third-grade-matters/.

Asl, Farshad. 2016. *The "No Excuses" Mindset: A Life of
Purpose, Passion, and Clarity*. Ohio: Author Academy
Elite.

Azzam, Amy M. 2014. "Motivated to Learn: A
Conversation with Daniel Pink." *Educational Leadership*
72 (1): 12–17.
http://www.ascd.org/publications/educational-
leadership/sept14/vol72/num01/Motivated-to-Learn@-A-
Conversation-with-Daniel-Pink.aspx.

Berger, Knute. 2013. "Seattle's Ugly Past: Segregation in
our Neighborhoods." *Seattle Magazine*.
https://www.seattlemag.com/article/seattles-ugly-past-
segregation-our-neighborhoods.

Bernard, Sarah. 2010. "Neuroplasticity: Learning
Physically Changes the Brain." Edutopia.

https://www.edutopia.org/neuroscience-brain-based-learning-neuroplasticity.

Bjork, Elizabeth, and Robert Bjork. n.d. "Applying Cognitive Psychology to Enhance Educational Practice." UCLA, Bjork Learning and Forgetting Lab. https://bjorklab.psych.ucla.edu/research/.

Bloom, Benjamin. 1956. *Taxonomy of Educational Objectives*. Chicago: University of Chicago.

Boaler, Jo. 2016. *Mathematical Mindsets: Unleashing Students' Potential through Creative Math, Inspiring Messages and Innovative Teaching*. San Francisco: Jossey-Bass.

Bowen, Janine. 2019. "Award-Winning Article Focuses on What It Means for Black Students to Belong at School." Black and Belonging, June 15. https://blackandbelonging.com/2019/06/13/award-winning-article-focuses-on-what-it-means-for-black-students-to-belong-at-school/.

Bridge International Academies. 2019. "How Important Is Literacy to Education and Development?" https://www.bridgeinternationalacademies.com/literacy-and-education/.

Brooks, Roger. Website: *Facing History and Ourselves*. Brookline, MA: https://www.facinghistory.org.

Brown, Brene. 2018. *Dare to Lead: Brave Work. Tough conversations. Whole hearts.* London: Vermilion.

Carter, Gene. 2012. Quote from Dr. Carter made at the 2012 ASCD "Whole Child Virtual Conference." http://www.wholechildeducation.org/blog/what-was-your-favorite-quote-from-wcvc12.

Clear, James. 2018. *Atomic Habits: An Easy & Proven Way to Build Good Habits & Break Bad Ones*. New York: Avery.

Close, Susan. n.d. "A Framework for Deeper Learning." https://www.smartlearning.ca/pdfs/Framework-for-deeper-learning-v2.pdf.

Collins, Jim. 2001. *Good to Great: Why Some Companies Make the Leap and Others Don't*. New York: HarperCollins.

Comaford, Christine. 2018. "Emotions Have Energy: What Energy Are You Sending?" *Forbes*, June 2. https://www.forbes.com/sites/christinecomaford/2018/06/02/emotions-have-energy-what-energy-are-you-sending/#694773142545.

Couros, George. 2015. *The Innovator's Mindset: Empower Learning, Unleash Talent, and Lead a Culture of Creativity*. San Diego, CA: Dave Burgess Consulting.

Covey, Stephen M. R. 2005. *The Speed of Trust: The One Thing That Changes Everything*. New York: Free Press.

Delvecchio, Jennifer, and Sharon Jeroski. 2016. *Changing Results for Young Readers Report 2012–2015.* British Columbia Ministry of Education. https://cr4yr.files.wordpress.com/2015/08/cr4yr_infographic.pdf.

Drago-Severson, Eleanor. 2008. *National Staff Development Council.* "4 Practices Serve as Pillars of Adult Learning." Vol. 29. No. 4.

———. 2009. *Leading Adult Learning: Supporting Adult Development in Our Schools.* New York: Corwin.

Duckworth, Angela. 2016. *Grit: The Power of Passion and Perseverance*. New York: Scribner.

Dweck, Carol S. 2017. *Mindset: Changing the Way You Think to Fulfil Your Potential*. London: Robinson.

Dweck, Carol S., Gregory M. Walton, and Geoffrey L. Cohen. 2014. *Academic Tenacity: Mindsets and Skills That Promote Long-Term Learning*. Bill & Melinda Gates Foundation. https://ed.stanford.edu/sites/default/files/manual/dweck-walton-cohen-2014.pdf.

Elliot, Jeffrey. 1989. *Conversations with Maya Angelou*. Mississippi: University Press of Mississippi.

Ericsson, K. Anders, Ralf T. Krampe, and Clemens Tesch-Römer. 1993. "The Role of Deliberate Practice in the Acquisition of Expert Performance." *Psychological Review* 100(3): 363–406. doi:10.1037//0033-295X.100.3.363.

Fox, Mem. 2008. *Reading Magic: Why Reading Aloud to Our Children Will Change Their Lives Forever*. New York: Harcourt Press.

Freeman, Tierra M., Lynley H. Anderman, and Jane M. Jensen. 2007. "Sense of Belonging in College Freshmen at the Classroom and Campus Levels." *Journal of Experimental Education 75* (3): 203–20. https://doi.org/10.3200/JEXE.75.3.203-220.

Fullan, Michael, and Geoff Scott. 2014. *Education PLUS: The World Will Be Led by People You Can Count on, Including You!* Seattle, Washington: Collaborative Impact SPC. https://documentcloud.adobe.com/link/review?uri=urn:aaid:scds:US:f1c87f39-a7c6-430b-9bf9-5adf1b438691 – 6 C's.

Gandhi, Jill. 2021. "Why I Am No Longer Using the Phrase "Achievement Gap": Perspective from an Educator and Developmental Psychologist." *Social Creatures*. https://www.thesocialcreatures.org/thecreaturetimes/opportunity-gap.

Gilbert, Lisa, Anne Teravainen, Christina Clark, and Sophia Shaw. 2018. "Literacy and Life Expectancy: An Evidence Review Exploring the Link between Literacy and Life Expectancy in England through Health and Socioeconomic Factors." National Literacy Trust Research Report. https://documentcloud.adobe.com/link/review?uri=urn:aaid :scds:US:fd2a21ab-b4ca-43b9-a738-b309a96626a1.

Gladwell, Malcolm. 2002. *The Tipping Point: How Little Things Can Make a Big Difference*. Boston/New York: Little, Brown and Company.

———. 2008. *Outliers: The Story of Success*. New York: Little, Brown and Company.

Goleman, Daniel. 2013. *Focus: The Hidden Driver of Excellence*. New York: Harper.

Gonser, Sarah. 2020. "4 Ways to Prioritize Relationships When Schools Reopen." Administration and Leadership. Edutopia, August 14. https://www.edutopia.org/article/4-ways-prioritize-relationships-when-schools-reopen.

Goodenow, Carol. 1993. "Classroom Belonging among Early Adolescent Students: Relationships to Motivation and Achievement." The Journal of Early Adolescence 1: (1): 21–43. https://doi.org/10.1177/0272431693013001002.

Gray, DeLeon L. 2018. "Is Psychological Membership in the Classroom a Function of Standing out While Fitting in? Implications for Achievement Motivation and Emotions." *Journal of School Psychology* 61:103–21. https://pubmed.ncbi.nlm.nih.gov/28259241/.

———. 2021. Interview by Janine Roy, January 14.

Gray, DeLeon L., Elan C. Hope, and Jamaal S. Matthews. 2018. "Black and Belonging at School: A Case for Interpersonal, Instructional, and Institutional Opportunity

Structures." *Educational Psychologist* 53 (2): 97–113. https://eric.ed.gov/?id=EJ1175609.

Greene, Ross W. 2014. *Lost at School: Why Our Kids with Behavioral Challenges Are Falling through the Cracks and How We Can Help Them.* New York: Scribner.

—. 2020. *Assessment of Lagging Skills & Unsolved Problems (ALSUP).* https://livesinthebalance.org/wp-content/uploads/2021/06/ALSUP-2020.pdf.

Hammond, Zaretta. 2015. *Culturally Responsive Teaching and the Brain: Promoting Authentic Engagement and Rigor among Culturally and Linguistically Diverse Students.* Thousand Oaks, CA: Corwin.

Hannah Jones, Nikole. Elliot, Mary. Huges, Jazmine. Silverstein, Jake. 2019. *The 1619 Project.* New York: New York Times Company. https://www.nytimes.com/interactive/2019/08/14/magazine/1619-america-slavery.html.

Hanushek, Eric A. 2016. "What Matters for Student Achievement." *Education Next* 16 (2). https://www.educationnext.org/what-matters-for-student-achievement/.

Hargreaves, Andy, and Michael Fullan. 2012. *Professional Capital: Transforming Teaching in Every School.* New York: Teachers College Press.

Hawkins, David R. 2013. *Power vs. Force: The Hidden Determinants to Human Behavior.* Carlsbad, CA/New York: Hay House.

Hebb, D.O. 1949. *The Organization of Behavior: A Neuropsychological Theory.* New York: John Wiley & Sons.

Hermans, Hubert J., and Frans Meijers. 2019. "The Pursuit of Happiness: Between Prosperity and Adversity." *British Journal of Guidance and Counselling* 47 (2): 139–42. https://www.tandfonline.com/doi/full/10.1080/03069885.2019.1612515?scroll=top&needAccess=true.

Hernandez, Donald. 2011. "Double Jeopardy: How Third-Grade Reading Skills and Poverty Influence High School Graduation." New York: Annie E. Casey Foundation. ERIC Number: ED518818. https://eric.ed.gov/?id=ED518818#:~:text=ERIC%20%2D%20ED518818%20%2D%20Double%20Jeopardy%3A,Casey%20Foundation%2C%202011%2DApr&text=Hernandez%2C%20Donald%20J.&text=Educators%20and%20researchers%20have%20long,the%20end%20of%20third%20grade.

Hobson, Jeremy. 2019. "Trevor Noah's Lesson to Young Readers: It's Freeing to Define Yourself on Your Own Terms." WBUR *Here and Now.* https://www.wbur.org/hereandnow/2019/06/04/trevor-noah-young-adult-born-a-crime.

Houck, Bonnie D., and Kari Ross. 2012. "Dismantling the Myth of Learning to Read and Reading to Learn." *Association for Supervision and Curriculum Development.* http://www.ascd.org/ascd-express/vol7/711-houck.aspx.

International Dyslexia Association. 2016. "Dyslexia Basics." https://dyslexiaida.org/dyslexia-basics/.

Inzlicht, Michael, Amitai Shenhav, and Christopher Y. Olivola. 2018. "The Effort Paradox: Effort Is Both Costly and Valued." *Trends in Cognitive Sciences* 22 (4): 337–49. doi: 10.1016/j.tics.2018.01.007.

Ishimaru, Ann M. 2014. "When New Relationships Meet Old Narratives: The Journey Towards Improving Parent-School Relations in a District-Community Organizing Collaboration." *Teachers College Record* 116. 0161-4681.

https://documentcloud.adobe.com/link/review?uri=urn:aaid
:scds:US:16e8442c-fb79-46f9-83d1-94efaf846ff3.

———.2017. "From Family Engagement to Equitable
Collaboration." *Educational Policy* 33 (2): 350–85.
https://journals.sagepub.com/doi/abs/10.1177/08959048176
91841.

———. 2020. *Just Schools: Building Equitable
Collaborations with Families and Communities*. New
York: Teachers College Press.

Jacobson, Linda. 2018. "Duckworth: 'Deliberate Practice'
Is an Important Element of Grit." K–12 Deep Dive.
Dive/Wire. April 18.
https://www.educationdive.com/news/duckworth-
deliberate-practice-is-an-important-element-of-
grit/521559/.

Joffe-Walt, Chana. 2020. *Nice White Parents. New York
Times* podcast.
https://www.nytimes.com/2020/07/23/podcasts/nice-white-
parents-serial.html.

Johnson, Pat, and Katie Keier. 2010. *Catching Readers
Before They Fall: Supporting Readers Who Struggle, K–4*.
New York: Stenhouse.

Johnson Hess, Abigail. 2018. "The 10 Most Educated
Countries in the World." CNBC. Small Business Playbook.
https://www.cnbc.com/2018/02/07/the-10-most-educated-
countries-in-the-
world.html#:~:text=Canada%20tops%20the%20list%20as,
of%20education%20after%20high%20school.

Juvonen, Jaana. 2007. "Reforming Middle Schools: Focus
on Continuity, Social Connectedness, and Engagement."
Educational Psychologist 42 (4):197–208.
doi:10.1080/00461520701621046.

Kendi, Ibram X. 2019. *How to Be an Antiracist.* New York: One World.

———. 2020. *Antiracist Baby*. New York: Kokila.

Kitchenham, Andrew. 2008. "The Evolution of John Mezirow's Transformative Learning Theory." *Journal of Transformative Education* 6 (2):104–23. http://dx.doi.org/10.1177/1541344608322678.

Koyier-Mwamba, Anita. 2020. Interview by Janine Roy, October 28.

Kromer, Suzanne V. 2017. "Seeking Mirrors: A Study of Student Selection and Use of Culturally Relevant Texts." *Boise State University Theses and Dissertations*. 1345. https://doi.org/10.18122/B21422.

Kuypers, Leah. 2011. *The Zones of Regulation: A Curriculum Designed to Foster Self-Regulation and Emotional Control.* Santa Clara, CA: Think Social.

Ladson-Billings, Gloria. 2014. "Culturally Relevant Pedagogy 2.0: a.k.a. the Remix." *Harvard Educational Review* 84 (1): 74–84. https://doi.org/10.17763/haer.84.1.p2rj131485484751.

The Latino Family Literacy Project. n.d. "What Does It Mean to Be Culturally Responsive?" Our Blog. https://www.latinoliteracy.com/mean-culturally-responsive/#:~:text=According%20to%20the%20National%20Center,and%20sustain%20a%20culturally%20responsive.

Levin, Ben. (2011). *Education Week.* "Comparing Canada and the U.S. on Education." https://www.edweek.org/education/opinion-comparing-canada-and-the-u-s-on-education/2011/04.

Linnenbrink-Garcia, Lisa, Erika A. Patall, and Reinhard Pekrun. 2016. "Adaptive Motivation and Emotion in Education: Research and Principles for Instructional Design." *Policy Insights from the Behavioral and Brain Sciences* 3 (2): 228–36. https://epub.ub.uni-muenchen.de/56690/.

The Literacy Project Foundation citing data compiled from *National Institute for Literacy, National Center for Adult Literacy, and U.S. Census Bureau. (2017).* https://www.literacyprojectfoundation.org/.

Long, Jennifer. 2016. "The Importance of Practice—and Our Reluctance to Do It." Harvard Business Publishing, April 27. https://www.harvardbusiness.org/the-importance-of-practice-and-our-reluctance-to-do-it/. In the article, she quotes Kaufman, Josh. 2010. *The Personal MBA: Master the Art of Business.* New York: Portfolio.

Love, Bettina. 2019. *We Want to Do More Than Survive: Abolitionist Teaching and the Pursuit of Educational Freedom.* New York: Beacon Press.

———.n.d. Website: *Abolitionist Teaching Network.* https://abolitionistteachingnetwork.org.

Mahadevan, Roopa. 2013. *Health Literacy Fact Sheets.* Center for Health Care Strategies. https://www.chcs.org/resource/health-literacy-fact-sheets/#:~:text=Nearly%2036%20percent%20of%20adults, income%20Americans%20eligible%20for%20Medicaid.

Maslow, Abraham H. 1943. "A Theory of Human Motivation." *Psychological Review* 50 (4): 370–96.

McCarthy, John E., and Saul A. Rubinstein. 2017. "National Study on Union-Management Partnerships and Educator Collaboration in US Public Schools." Cornell University: Collaborative School Leadership Initiative Working Paper.

https://documentcloud.adobe.com/link/review?uri=urn:aaid :scds:US:27d14d03-3609-4717-b5fe-5b1a34b9c186.

McGhee, Heather. 2020. *The Sum of Us: What Racism Costs Everyone and How We Can Prosper Together.* New York: One World.

Montessori, Maria. (1912). *The Montessori Method: Scientific Pedagogy as Applied to Child Education in the Children's Houses: English Edition.* New York: Frederick A. Stokes Company.

Montoya, Silvia. 2018. *Defining Literacy.* UNESCO Institute for Statistics. http://gaml.uis.unesco.org/wp-content/uploads/sites/2/2018/12/4.6.1_07_4.6-defining-literacy.pdf.

Muhammad, Gholdy. 2020. *Cultivating Genius: An Equity Framework for Culturally and Historically Responsive Literacy.* New York: Scholastic.

Nasir, Na'ilah Suad, Jarvis R. Givens, and Christopher P. Chatmon, eds. 2018. *"We Dare Say Love": Supporting Achievement in the Educational Life of Black Boys.* New York/London: Teachers College Press.

NCES (National Center for Educational Statistics). (2017). "Education Expenditures by Country." https://nces.ed.gov/programs/coe/indicator/cmd.

———. (2018). "Racial/Ethnic Enrollment in Public Schools." https://nces.ed.gov/programs/coe/indicator/cge.

———. 2019a. U.S. Department of Education. "Digest of Education Statistics: 2009 Tables and Figures." https://nces.ed.gov/programs/digest/d09/tables/dt09_050.asp.

———. 2019b. U.S. Department of Education. "Datapoints." https://nces.ed.gov/datapoints/2019179.asp.

———. 2019c. U.S. Department of Education. "Fast Facts: Adult Literacy." Cites 2014 Program for International Assessment of Adult Competencies (PIAAC) Literacy Framework. https://nces.ed.gov/fastfacts/display.asp?id=69.

———. February 2019d. "Status and Trends in the Education of Racial and Ethnic Groups: Indicator 27: Educational Attainment." https://nces.ed.gov/programs/raceindicators/indicator_RFA.asp.

———. 2020. "Public High School Graduation Rates." Condition of Education—Preprimary, Elementary, and Secondary Education. https://nces.ed.gov/programs/coe/indicator_coi.asp.

Nelsen, Jane. 2006. *Positive Discipline: The Classic Guide to Helping Children Develop Self-Discipline, Responsibility, Cooperation, and Problem-Solving Skills*. New York: Ballantine.

Nelson, Nella. 2021. Interview by Janine Roy, June 1.

November, Alan. 2012. *Who Owns the Learning? Preparing Students for Success in the Digital Age*, 2nd ed. Bloomington, IN: Solution Tree Press.

OECD (Organization for Economic Cooperation and Development). 2013. *"OECD Skills Outlook 2013: First Results from the Survey of Adult Skills."* OECD iLibrary. https://www.oecd-ilibrary.org/education/oecd-skills-outlook-2013_9789264204256-en.

Payne, Wendy. 2021. Interview by Janine Roy, May 30.

Piaget, Jean. 1966. *The Psychology of the Child.* New York: Perseus Books.

Poff Roman, Sarah. 2010. "Illiteracy and Older Adults: Individual and Societal Implications." *Educational Gerontology* 30 (2): 79–93. https://www.tandfonline.com/doi/abs/10.1080/0360127049 0266257. doi: 10.1080/03601270490266257.
Positive Discipline. n.d. Mistaken Goal Chart. https://www.positivediscipline.com/sites/default/files/mista kengoalchart.pdf.

Prenger, Rilana, Cindy L. Poortman, and Adam Handelzalts. 2020. "Professional Learning Networks: From Teacher Learning to School Improvement?" *Journal of Educational Change* 22: 13–52. https://link.springer.com/article/10.1007/s10833-020-09383-2#Sec1.

Ranseth, Joseph. 2015. "Gandhi Didn't Actually Ever Say 'Be the Change You Want to See in the World.' Here's the Real Quote…" Joseph Ranseth website, August 24. https://josephranseth.com/gandhi-didnt-say-be-the-change-you-want-to-see-in-the-world/.

Rea, Amy. 2020. *Library Journal.* "How Serious Is America's Literacy Problem?" https://www.libraryjournal.com/?detailStory=How-Serious-Is-Americas-Literacy-Problem.

Reeve, Johnmarshall. 2009. "Why Teachers Adopt a Controlling Motivating Style toward Students and How They Can Become More Autonomy Supportive." *Educational Psychologist* 44 (3):159–75. https://www.researchgate.net/publication/240240910_Why _Teachers_Adopt_a_Controlling_Motivating_Style_Towar d_Students_and_How_They_Can_Become_More_Autono my_Supportive.

Reich, Justin, and Jal Mehta. 2020. "Imagining September: Principles and Design Elements for Ambitious Schools During COVID-19." EdArXiv Preprints, July 3. https://doi.org/10.35542/osf.io/gqa2w.

Richardson, John, and Douglas Judge. 2013. "The Intergroup Dynamics of a Metaphor: The School-to-Prison Pipeline." Journal of Educational Controversy 7 (1).

Riley, Richard W., and Terry K. Peterson. 2008. "Before the 'Either-Or' Era: Reviving Bipartisanship to Improve America's Schools." *Education Week.* See Annie E Casey report, footnote 2.

Ritchhart, Ron. 2015. *Creating Cultures of Thinking: The 8 Forces We Must Master to Truly Transform Our Schools.* San Francisco: Jossey-Bass.

Roach, Marjorie I. 2021. Interview by Janine Roy, April 15.

Roser, Max, and Esteban Ortiz-Ospina. 2018. "Literacy." OurWorldInData.org. https://ourworldindata.org/literacy.

Ryan, Camille, and Kurt Bauman. 2016. "Educational Attainment in the United States: 2015." United States Census Bureau. https://www.census.gov/library/publications/2016/demo/p20-578.html.

Safir, Shane, and Jamila Dugan. 2021. *Street Data: A Next-Generation Model for Equity, Pedagogy, and School Transformation.* New York: Corwin.

Scarborough, H. S. 2001. "Connecting Early Language and Literacy to Later Reading (Dis)abilities: Evidence, Theory, and Practice." In S. Neuman and D. Dickinson (eds.), *Handbook for Research in Early Literacy* (pp. 97–110). New York: Guilford Press.

https://dyslexiaida.org/scarboroughs-reading-rope-a-groundbreaking-infographic/.

Scarlett, Keisha. 2020. Interview by Janine Roy, November 5.

Schmoker, Mike. 2011. *Focus: Elevating the Essentials to Radically Improve Student Learning*, 2nd ed. Alexandria, VA: ASCD.

Seattle Public Schools. n.d. https://www.seattleschools.org/departments/strategy_and_partnerships.

Seattle Public Schools. n.d. Policy 0030: African American Male Achievement. Website. https://www.seattleschools.org/wp-content/uploads/2021/07/0030.pdf.

Sessoms, Gail. n.d. "Effects of Illiteracy on Business." *Houston Chronicle.* https://smallbusiness.chron.com/effects-illiteracy-business-22898.html.

Shanker, Stuart. 2012. *Calm, Alert, and Learning: Classroom Strategies for Self-Regulation.* Toronto: Pearson Education Canada.

Siegel, Daniel J., and Tina Payne Bryson. 2011. *The Whole-Brain Child: 12 Revolutionary Strategies to Nurture Your Child's Developing Mind.* New York: Delacorte.

Sinclair, Murray. 2015. "Canadian Commission Releases 'Damning' Report on Treatment of Aboriginal Children." NPR Morning Edition interview, June 4. https://www.npr.org/2015/06/04/411917428/canadian-commission-releases-damning-report-on-treatment-of-aboriginal-children.

"Social Dynamics of Energy Behaviour." 2020. *Nature Energy* 5: 179. https://doi.org/10.1038/s41560-020-0595-8.

Social Justice Tool Box. n.d. "Privilege for Sale." https://www.socialjusticetoolbox.com/activity/privilege-for-sale/.

Society for Neuroscience. 2004. "Dyslexia: What Brain Research Reveals about Reading." LD Online. http://www.ldonline.org/article/10784/#:~:text=Dyslexia%20occurs%20among%20people%20of,%2C%20writing%2C%20and%20spelling%20difficulties.

Somers, Stephen A., and Roopa Mahadevan. 2010. *Health Literacy Implications of the Affordable Care Act*. Center for Health Care Strategies. https://www.chcs.org/resource/health-literacy-implications-of-the-affordable-care-act/.

Sparks, Sarah D. 2011. "Study: Third Grade Reading Predicts High School Graduation." *Education Week*, April 8. http://blogs.edweek.org/edweek/inside-school-research/2011/04/the_disquieting_side_effect_of.html.

Spector, Carrie. 2019. "'Embrace the struggle': Stanford Education Professor Challenges Common Beliefs about Teaching and Learning." *Stanford News*, September 30. https://news.stanford.edu/2019/09/30/embrace-struggle-education-professor-challenges-common-beliefs-teaching-learning/.

Statistics Canada. 2016a. "Population and Dwelling Count Highlight Tables, 2016 Census." https://www12.statcan.gc.ca/census-recensement/2016/dp-pd/hlt-fst/pd-pl/Table.cfm?Lang=Eng&T=101&S=50&O=A.

———. (2016b). "Visible Minorities, among the School Age Population, in and out of Census Metropolitan Areas (CMAs)."

https://www150.statcan.gc.ca/t1/tbl1/en/tv.action?pid=3710
009803.

————. 2020. "Canada's Black Population: Education,
Labour and Resilience." Ethnicity, Language and
Immigration Thematic Series.
https://www150.statcan.gc.ca/n1/pub/89-657-x/89-657-
x2020002-eng.htm.

Summit Academy. 2016. "Newton's Three Laws with a
Bicycle." Video.
https://draper.summitacademyschools.org/apps/video/watch
.jsp?v=112055.

Toldson, Ivory A. 2019. *No BS (Bad Stats): Black People
Need People Who Believe in Black People Enough Not to
Believe Every Bad Thing They Hear about Black People.*
Boston: Brill Sense.

Truman Center for National Policy. 2013. "Illiteracy Costs
the Global Economy $1 Trillion."
http://trumancenter.org/doctrine-blog/illiteracy-costs-the-
global-economy-1-
trillion/#:~:text=The%20effects%20of%20illiteracy%20%5
Binclude,expensive%20for%20too%20many%20countries.

UNESCO (United Nations Educational, Scientific and
Cultural Organization). n.d. "Literacy."
https://en.unesco.org/themes/literacy.

United Nations. 1997. "Secretary-General Stresses Need
for Political Will and Resources to Meet Challenge of Fight
against Illiteracy." United Nations. Meetings Coverage and
Press Releases, United Nations Literacy Day.
https://www.un.org/press/en/1997/19970904.SGSM6316.ht
ml#:~:text=Following%20is%20the%20message%20of,dai
ly%20life%20in%20modern%20society.

U.S. Census Bureau. 2019. "Quick Facts." https://www.census.gov/quickfacts/fact/table/US/PST0452 19.

Valentine, Maryann. 1999. *The Reggio Emilia Approach to Early Learning Education.* Scotland: Scottish Consultative Council on the Curriculum.

Wexler, Natalie. 2018. "Why American Students Haven't Gotten Better at Reading in 20 Years." *The Atlantic*, April 13. https://www.theatlantic.com/education/archive/2018/04/-american-students-reading/557915/.

Weyer, Matthew, and Jorge E. Casares. 2019. "Pre-Kindergarten–Third Grade Literacy." National Conference of State Legislators Newsletter, December.

Wigfield, Allan, Jessica Gladstone, and Lara Turci. 2016. "Beyond Cognition: Reading Motivation and Reading Comprehension." *Child Development Perspectives 10* (3): 190–95. https://www.ncbi.nlm.nih.gov/pmc/articles/PMC5014370/.

Wikipedia. 2021. "List of Countries by Total Wealth." Credit Suisse data. https://en.wikipedia.org/wiki/List_of_countries_by_total_wealth.

Wilkerson, Isabel. 2020. *Caste: The Origins of Our Discontents.* New York: Random House.

World Literacy Foundation. n.d. https://worldliteracyfoundation.org/.

World Population Review. 2022. "Richest Countries in the World 2022." https://worldpopulationreview.com/country-rankings/richest-countries-in-the-world.

Books on How to *Actually* Teach Reading: It is essential for educators to identify research-based resources for teaching this complex life skill. There is a multitude of brilliant research-based literacy instruction resources for teachers. The section below includes some of my favorites:

Muhammad, Gholdy. 2020. *Cultivating Genius: An Equity Framework for Culturally and Historically Responsive Literacy*. New York: Scholastic.

Serravallo, Jennifer. 2015. *The Reading Strategies Book: Your Everything Guide to Developing Skilled Readers*. Portsmouth, NH: Heinemann.

———. 2017. *The Writing Strategies Book: Your Everything Guide to Developing Skilled Writers*. NH: Heinemann.

Johnson, Pat, and Katie Keier. 2010. *Catching Readers Before They Fall: Supporting Readers Who Struggle, K–4*. New York: Stenhouse.

Miller, Debbie. 2018. *What's the Best That Could Happen?: New Possibilities for Teachers &Readers*. Portsmouth, NH, Heinemann.

Ziemke, Kristin, and Katie Muhtaris. 2019. *Read the World: Rethinking Literacy for Empathy and Action in a Digital Age*. Portsmouth, NH: Heinemann.

Allington, Richard L. 1996. (Reposted 1/2/2018.) "The Six Ts of Effective Elementary Literacy Instruction." Washington: AdLit.Org. https://www.staffordschools.net/site/handlers/filedownload.ashx?moduleinstanceid=3573&dataid=49014&FileName=The%20Six%20Ts%20of%20Effective%20Elementary%20Literacy%20Instruction%20Reading%20Rockets.pdf.

———. 2011. *What Really Matters for Struggling Readers: Designing Research-Based Programs*, 3rd ed. Boston: Pearson.

Children's books referenced in *Momentum:*

Angelou, Maya. 1996. *Kofi and His Magic.* New York: Random House Children's Books.

———.1994. *My Painted House, My Friendly Chicken and Me.* New York: Random House Children's Books.

———.1993. *Life Doesn't Frighten Me.* New York: Random House Children's Books.

Brown, Monica. 2015. *Lola Levine is Not Mean.* New York: Hachette Book Group.

Caldecott, Randolph. 1877. *This is the House that Jack Built.* London: *The Morning Chronicle.*

Dean, James. 2010. *Pete the Cat: I Love My White Shoes.* New York: HarperCollins.

Gray, William. 1946. *Fun with Dick and Jane.* New York: Penguin.

Keats, Ezra Jack. 1996. *The Snowy Day.* New York: Penguin.

Kendi, Ibram X. 2020. *Antiracist Baby.* New York: Kokila.

Lobel, Arnold. 1970. *Frog and Toad are Friends.* New York: HarperCollins.

Maslen, Bobby Lynn. 1973. *Bob Books.* New York: Scholastic.

Reynolds, Jason, and Ibram X. Kendi. 2021. *Stamped (for Kids): Racism, Antiracism and You.* New York: Hachette Book Group.

Seuss, Dr. 1957. *The Cat in the Hat.* New York: Random House for Young Readers.

Weinman Sharmot, Marjorie. 1977. *Nate the Great.* New York: Yearling.

Willems, Mo. 2007. *There Is a Bird on Your Head.* New York: Hyperion Books for Children.

White, E.B. 1952. *Charlotte's Web.* New York: Harper Collins.

Acknowledgments

I must begin by openly acknowledging the layered privileges I have been afforded. As a white Canadian who grew up in a middle-class home in Victoria, B.C., Canada, currently working as an elementary school principal in the United States, it has been my privilege to not have to think about my race for most of my life. Being able to confidently declare my identity as an avid reader, educator, and critical thinker "to better understand the truth in history, power and equity" (Muhammad 2020) are all profound privileges I have been blessed with as a white Canadian female. My own ignorance is shameful and must be corrected, and I aim to spend the rest of my life striving to learn, and to support and empower every student, especially those students and families farthest from educational justice. As it is foundational to begin the essential shift from a caste-based society to an equity-based community, acknowledging my privilege is an essential component of twenty-first century North American society (Wilkerson 2020).

The purpose of this book was to honor and support the right of every child to have the same privileges I had: the right to feel belonging and build trust with the adults around them so they can learn to read. Every kid needs these privileges so that they grow up being the critical thinkers and social justice champions our twenty-first century society needs them to be.

I am so grateful to my family who supported me in the writing of this book:

First and foremost, I so appreciate the love and support of my husband, Robert. At the start of the pandemic, while I scrambled to support my students, staff, and their families, my non-educator husband urged me to write this book. I am forever grateful to my best friend, collaborative partner, tireless editor, and wise life coach. He read every draft. Again and again. That's love.

Thank-you to my son, Matt, and his wife, Devi. As special education teachers in Canada, they brought a joyful collaborative partnership to this work, and I thank them for their wise insights, thoughtful feedback, and partnership as we move forward together as both family and colleagues. They bravely read through my very rough first drafts. Their wise educator insights shaped this book.

My daughter Hayley was a huge inspiration for this book. She opened my eyes to the complex journey of growing up as an African American in Canada. Now living in America, Hayley makes me so proud and broadens my White-centric horizons daily as this inspiring Queen faces microaggressions and outright racism with Black Excellence and determination. Her joie de vivre and grit are inspiring.

I will always be grateful to my parents, Margaret and Ray Bryant, who taught me that I could do anything I put my mind to. Early in my career, my mom and I took university classes together, taught workshops together on technology and literacy, and collaborated on endless literacy initiatives as we both taught Third Grade in Victoria, B.C., Canada. Fundamentally, she taught me everything I know about creating belonging and trust in a family, in my classroom, and in the world around me. Gracious and giving throughout her life, she passed away as I completed the final edits for this book. She will always be my hero and mentor.

Thank you to my brothers, Michael and Alan, for teaching me about belonging, determination, service, the importance of laughter, and the power of love.

I so appreciate my sister-in-law Gail Roy for her wise advice and support on the cover design.

Many thanks to my editors, as they helped me to transform my 'baby' into reality. Thank you to my brilliant developmental editor, Nancy Cortelyou. You brought your skill, wisdom, and joy to editing this work. Huge thanks to Paul Tabili, my copy editor. Your phenomenal attention to detail and skilful reference checking were greatly appreciated!

A huge thanks to my colleagues, past and present. Each year, the humans in my school community give me a new year of learning and growth. As I've been in the education business for 38 years, I've worked with and learned from a lot of humans!

Thank-you to my Canadian teacher and administrator colleagues in the Greater Victoria School District from Northridge Elementary, Rogers Elementary, George Jay Elementary, Arbutus Global Middle School, and Central Office.

In Seattle, many thanks to my Queen Anne Elementary colleagues, past and present, who have taught me so much. I can't thank you enough for your collaboration and partnership. Special thanks to teachers Lorin Belcher, Mike Backman, Rachel Scheer, and Dr. Liz David for sharing their feedback on my early drafts. Thank-you to my Seattle Public Schools Directors over the past six years: Dr. Sarah Pritchett, Dr. Kelly Aramaki, Heather Eberts, and Dr. Jim Mercer. Your leadership and wisdom taught me a great deal and cultivated my professional joy.

In Victoria, thank you to former-teacher-buddies-and-dear-friends for sharing your invaluable feedback and wisdom. Marjorie Roach, my forever teaching partner and best friend, thank you for being the Best Reading Teacher I've ever met. Your insights about the power of Home Reading inspired past and present reading initiatives. Wendy Payne, thank you for actually teaching me how to teach reading and continuing to mentor me to this day. Your research-based, SEL-informed instructional practices impacted reading programs in many schools, and your leadership as a principal taught me the value of being a literacy-centered principal. Colleen Neves, thank you for your wise input as an experienced First Grade teacher, brilliant colleague, and dear friend.

I am very grateful to my friends for their encouragement and help. Dr. Kayla Young and husband Jesse Young, I am forever thankful for your kind feedback on my first drafts, which was so helpful and so brave because my first drafts were awful! Thank-you to Jesse Young for partnering on creating a nonprofit for Momentum to support young readers farthest from educational justice. Huge thanks to dear friends Dr. Helen Campbell and Bill Erving, who taught me about the powerful impact of being loving parents, passionate global citizens, and enthusiastic 4-H Leaders and community members. I appreciated their support so much! Thank-you to my Victoria Book Club Sisters and my Seattle Book Club Buddies. Their encouragement was powerful!

I was very fortunate to interview several people for this book:

- Enormous thanks to Seattle Public Schools Assistant Superintendent of Academics Dr. Keisha Scarlett for her invaluable knowledge, wisdom, and insights. Throughout my years in Seattle Public Schools, she has been an inspirational educational leader, innovative educator, and wise mentor. In the midst of the global pandemic, she gave me time for an interview to learn more about her doctoral work on momentum. She also kindly gave me space to share my dreams and ideas and guided me to connect with Dr. DeLeon Gray and examine the research of Dr. Na'ilah Suad Nasir, Dr. Ellie Drago-Severson, Dr. Ann Ishimaru, and Dr. Ivory Toldson. She inspires educators and myself to stay laser-focused on loving every child and helping every child learn, while simultaneously leading our district's systemic shifts to equitably meet the needs of African American boys and students farthest from educational justice. She builds our individual and collective momentum every day. Her insights had a profound impact on my work.

- Huge appreciation to Dr. DeLeon Gray, Associate Professor at North Carolina State University, for allowing me to interview him on his research on belonging. I was also honored to be invited to meet with and learn from his doctoral students. Dr. Gray's powerful feedback, and the wisdom of his doctoral students, was inspiring. His powerful research on belonging became integral to Momentum.

- Endless gratitude to my colleague and friend, Seattle Public Schools Project-Program Manager for Black Studies, Anita Koyier-Mwamba, who allowed me to interview her about the powerful impact of family partnerships on student learning. She encouraged me to become a co-facilitator of North Seattle College's Family Connectors University course. Through many collaborations, she became my dear friend. I am blessed and grateful to continue our collaborative planning together. Her wisdom and insights helped to shape the family partnership elements of this book.

- I'm very grateful to 6-year-old Austin, a First Grade student at my school, who allowed me to interview him for this book. I partnered with his family and followed his reading journey during our first pandemic year and was thrilled to support him to get up the Learning to Read Hill.

It was a gift to watch his growing determination and reading joy!

I wouldn't be here today without a few incredible humans who helped me along my learning journey:

- Bob Warren changed my life. Long-time inspiring Canadian librarian at George Jay Elementary in Victoria, B.C., he became my vice principal when I assumed my first principalship. He developed "Read for the Top"[20] with his teaching partner, Bob Gretsinger. He introduced the concept of expanding our school's literacy initiatives to include a Home Reading Program, and we worked together on many schoolwide literacy initiatives. As an award-winning coach, he partnered with me to focus on belonging for our students farthest from educational justice. Within five years, our school shifted from one of the lowest performing schools in the province to the most improved school in the province in reading. He then very kindly nominated me for a

---

[20] Loosely based on the Reach for the Top game show, Bob and his teaching partner, Bob Gretsinger, created "Read for the Top." Using Canadian fiction and nonfiction, they set up teams, helped students to develop questions about each book, and set up a school wide reading competition to develop reading comprehension, build belonging, and galvanize learning momentum.

national principal award. Thank you for being an inspiring teacher, collaborative administrative partner, community volunteer, and dear friend.

- Thank-you to past administrative partners who taught me about leading with empathy and compassion. School Principals Trevor Calkins and Chris Harvey both taught me so much, guided me as a teacher and school administrator, and supported every initiative I cooked up. Thank you for being such wonderful mentors.

Thank-you to Canadian district leaders I've learned from and partnered with:

- Special thanks to Nella Nelson, Klaapalasugwela/Maxwagila, a Kwakwaka'wakw teacher, leader, mentor, advocate, mother, and grandmother, visionary school district leader, collaborative partner, and friend. Nella and her husband Alex Nelson taught me so much about the powerful impact of culturally responsive teaching and restorative justice.

- Eileen Eby, my mentor, fellow collaborator, and friend, showed me that professional pivots are possible and fun! Her leadership of district- and

297

community-based literacy initiatives continues to inspire me.

- The Late Dr. John Fawcett was a thoughtful colleague, wise mentor, and caring friend. His advice and insights were brilliant and always helpful.

- Many thanks to Greater Victoria School District Superintendent Deb Whitten for her collaboration and partnership on so many impactful initiatives.

- Huge appreciation to GVSD's former Director of Informational Technology Ted Pennell, now Chief Communications Officer at Victoria's Camosun College, for teaming on many creative projects.

- I would not be sitting in Seattle today if it was not for Canadian educational leaders Sherri Bell, Maureen Dockendorf, Mike McKay, Chris Harvey, and George Ambeault. These wonderful humans wrote letters in support of my American 0-1 Visa application, documenting my work as a principal and district leader. I am forever grateful for their incredible support in helping me make my dreams come true.

Huge thanks to all of you!

About the Author

Janine Roy is an award-winning school principal, author, speaker and experienced educational leader in both the United States and Canada. She is author of *Momentum,* and the companion book for parents, *Momentum Family Guide: Empowering Your Child's Learning While Maintaining Your Sanity and Sense of Humor.* Today, she is Professional Development Manager for Seattle Public Schools, professional development facilitator, and co-facilitator at North Seattle College. She lives with her husband in Seattle, Washington, and is the very proud mother of two grown children and one perfect grandson. To contact the author, go to https://www.janineroy.com/.

Lightning Source UK Ltd.
Milton Keynes UK
UKHW020747281122
412969UK00015B/2842